BIRDWATCHING
IN THE
LAKE DISTRICT

'He is the melancholy that flies
in the weathers of my mind . . .'

BIRDWATCHING
IN THE
LAKE DISTRICT

A BARTHOLOMEW MAP & GUIDE

BY MIKE MADDERS ILLUSTRATED BY PHILIP SNOW

JOHN BARTHOLOMEW & SON LTD EDINBURGH

British Library Cataloguing in Publication Data

Madders, Mike
  Birdwatching in the Lake District
  1. Bird watching—England—Lake District
  I. Title
  598'.07'2344278   QL690.G7

ISBN 0-7028-0762-1
Published and Printed in Scotland
by John Bartholomew & Son Ltd.
Duncan Street, Edinburgh EH9 1TA

The physical landscape of Britain is changing all the time,
e.g. as new tracks are made, hedges grubbed up and fields
amalgamated. While every care has been taken in the
preparation of this guide, the author and John Bartholomew & Son Ltd. will
not be responsible for any loss, damage or inconvenience
caused by inaccuracies.

B099

Dedicated to Princess Eleonora of Arborea c.1350-1403

CONTENTS

Ravens/Harter fell.
Eskdale ©

INTRODUCTION

There are two main aims to this book; firstly to describe the variety of bird habitats to be found in the Lake District and secondly to set out a personal selection of birdwatching localities which will enable the visiting birder to sample prime examples of each habitat. In doing so, given reasonable luck, he or she should encounter many of the birds typical of Lakeland without having to waste time in exploring less suitable areas.

The book is divided roughly into two sections, dealing with each of these aims in turn. I have avoided any attempt to give identification guidance, as this is well covered in the various field guides available. A systematic list of birds recorded in Cumbria since 1900 and a summary of their status is given at the back of the book.

I do not believe that only what is 'grey and boring' can be scientific, but in striving for accuracy an analytical style is occasionally unavoidable and to balance this I have relied heavily upon Philip's superb illustrations. These convey far better than words the inherent beauty of Lakeland's birdlife.

MIKE MADDERS
Gill Bank Cottage, 1985

It has been a great pleasure to work with Mike and to know that our many field trips, which have both expanded and refined my birding knowledge and illustrative technique, have finally evolved into this book.

As already noted, a certain air of informality and personal experience pervades the work and I hope that my drawings can likewise convey something of the magical appeal of Lakeland's diverse birds and habitats. This appeal often rests on the birds' inseperable relationships with their distinctive surroundings, echoed sublimely in their infinitely varied and often cryptic plumages; this has certainly influenced my portrayal of them. I can never, for instance, see Dippers without noticing the complex rock and water patterns that invariably accompany them, and Lakeland will never lack for water, in all its varied incarnations!

Obviously, one cannot hope to define such a varied region in the relatively few years and pages that were at my disposal, therefore I hope this can be seen as an introduction, an invitation to walk and sit quietly, to enjoy the superb birds and landscape of the Lakes.

PHILIP SNOW
Malltraeth, Anglesey, 1985

SOME INFORMATION FOR VISITORS

When to visit
Visitors with school-age children will have a very restricted choice as to when they can take their holidays in the Lake District and most arrive in July and August, generally a poor time of year for seeing Lakeland's birdlife. There is much to see and do at any time of year, of course, but given a free choice I would not hesitate to recommend the months of May and June, when the breeding birds tend to be more conspicuous in plumage, voice and behaviour.

Where to stay
There is a wide spectrum of accommodation available in Lakeland, from campsites to 5-star hotels, and the best advice I can offer here is to consult one of the many Tourist Information Centres in the area, where full details of local accommodation can be found. A list of these Centres is obtainable from the Cumbria Tourist Board at Windermere (*see* Addresses).

The most useful centres for Lakeland exploration are the popular Ambleside, Grasmere, Langdale and Keswick areas; yet these are, to my mind, less attractive than some of the remoter dales and you may well decide to choose one of these as a base and concentrate on one particular area rather than trying to cover the whole National Park. As I live in western Lakeland, I am inevitably biased in favour of the relatively unspoilt dales here, in particular Dunnerdale, Eskdale, Wasdale, Loweswater and Buttermere, although the lakes in this area are less interesting ornithologically than most. As a compromise, I would recommend the Ullswater, Coniston and Borrowdale valleys as worthy of consideration, since they all contain a good mix of habitats within a comparatively small area.

Transport
Public transport in the Lake District, as one would expect, is rather limited outside the main towns and popular visitor centres. Cumbria's rail 'network' comprises The Lakes Line, from Oxenholme (near Kendal) to Windermere, and the scenic Furness Line from Lancaster to Barrow, from where the West Cumbria Line leads to Whitehaven and then Carlisle. To the east lies the mainline Lancaster-Penrith-Carlisle line which climbs over Shap Summit.

Two main bus companies serve the area: Cumberland Motor Services Ltd and Ribble (*see* Addresses). Details of route numbers are given where applicable for each birdwatching locality described in the second half of this book. In addition, there are several small and sometimes unconventional transport operators which can be of use to visiting birders; for example the Ravenglass and Eskdale narrow gauge railway, the Mountain Goat minibus service, the Post Bus services, and the Lake Steamers on Windermere, Coniston Water, Ullswater and Derwentwater. It is therefore possible, if occasionally tedious, to reach most corners of Lakeland using public transport, and I would again recommend that you make enquiries at one of the Tourist Information Centres.

I feel that it is a fair assumption, however, that most visiting birders will be travelling by car, and the relevant distances and car parking details are given for each of the 22 sites.

Weather

Good weather is a gamble at any time of year and the only accurate statement that can be made about Lakeland weather is that it is generally unpredictable. The low cloud and rain that keep fellwalkers grounded, however, need not deter the birder, who can still explore the valley areas or make for the coast, where the worst weather often produces some of the most exciting birds. A detailed weather forecast is recorded daily by the Fell Top Weather Service (Tel. Windermere 5151) and this includes information on cloud base level, conditions underfoot, etc. For people venturing onto the mountains the importance of being aware of approaching bad weather, and having adequate equipment to deal with it, is continually stressed by Mountain Rescue Teams, the National Park Ranger Service and many other authorities, yet every year tragedies still occur due to some people's failure to heed this advice or to act with common sense. There is hardly a book written about Lakeland which does not carry dire warnings about the potential severity of mountain weather and recommend such a vast list of essential equipment that it is a wonder that anyone still dares to set foot on the fells, but even this does not seem to prevent a few foolhardy individuals from pushing their luck. There is no getting away from the fact that warm and waterproof clothing is essential, even if most of it spends all day in your rucksack. Strong footwear with good traction is obviously important too, although new designs and the use of lighter materials in recent years have meant that there is no longer any need to hobble around in a heavy pair of clumsy walking boots, unless that is what you prefer; good quality mountain boots weighing little more than a pair of training shoes are now widely available at outdoor shops throughout the Lake District and elsewhere. Also required are compass and map (the Ordnance Survey 1:25,000 Outdoor Leisure maps are ideal), whistle, some extra food such as chocolate, dates or Kendal Mint Cake, which will restore energy quickly, a modest first aid kit and a small rucksack in which to carry it all. From October through to April, I would add a woollen hat, a torch, and a survival bag to that list. Two useful items, often overlooked in the panic to be prepared for the worst possible weather conditions, are sun tan oil and midge repellent; a sun hat can be useful too on very hot days, and DON'T forget your binoculars!

If possible, leave word of your intended route and the estimated time of your return; do not press on if conditions are against you—turn back, even if this upsets your plans.

The foregoing advice is for the benefit of all those intending to venture onto the fells; for visiting the sites detailed later in this book your usual birdwatching attire will suffice. My preference in footwear would be for a pair of lightweight walking boots for all but the coastal and mire habitats, where wellingtons may be more suitable. A telescope is extremely useful for all areas of open water and I now find a tripod-mounted 'scope almost indispensable for water bird observation.

Finally, can I reiterate a piece of very well-aired advice: without doubt, the early morning is the optimum time to see most birds, particularly woodland species, and this is especially relevant in the Lake District where even popular tourist attractions can remain deserted until 8 or 9 a.m. In spring and summer I much prefer to be out just after first light and return by mid-morning to leave the place to the crowds.

Peregrine Falcon

MOUNTAIN AND MOORLAND

The Lake District comprises a radiating system of deep glacial valleys, interspersed with sharp peaks and narrow ridges. These valleys are characterised by sheer rock buttresses, long steep slopes of unstable scree, and fast-flowing mountain streams. So compressed is this jagged landscape that few large areas of open fell exist—notably the peripheral moorlands 'back o' Skiddaw', the Shap fells, or the afforested plateau of Grizedale.

Topographically, there are three main upland regions. To the south lie relatively soft sandstones supporting a predominantly moorland vegetation of heather, dwarf shrubs, grassland and bracken. By contrast, central Lakeland consists of hard volcanic rock types which have weathered to produce rugged mountains with extremely varied vegetation, although for the most part the slopes are grassy sheepwalk interspersed with bracken. The smoother contours of the Skiddaw fells typify the ancient slates and mudstones underlying northern Lakeland. Here one finds quite extensive areas of moorland with more heather cover than is usual in the Lake District, although grassland tends to predominate towards the western fells of the Grasmoor massif.

Most fellwalkers inevitably focus their attention upon the ascent of Lakeland's peaks, but the summits themselves, however fine their prospect, hold little to interest the naturalist and it is the diversity of the rugged fellsides with their many fine crags that will excite the birder's enthusiasm. The names of crags often reveal their past association with birds—Raven Crags abound and many are still tenanted by these birds centuries later. Eagle and Falcon Crags are similarly of obvious derivation, whilst Heron or Iron Crags probably denote the former site of an Erne, or Sea Eagle eyrie.

Lakeland's hill country is generally given over to sheep grazing and the impoverishment of the vegetation by these hardy herbivores causes the uplands to have rather limited bird communities. On the other hand, the birds that are to be found are often of considerable interest because of their comparative rarity elsewhere in Britain, and sheep farming does, of course, benefit carrion-eating birds such as Raven, Buzzard and Golden Eagle.

Crags

It is important for us to realise that the birds a hillwalker may encounter during an August day in the Coniston Fells will be quite different from those seen in the depths of winter by his duvet-clad counterpart, possibly struggling in near arctic conditions. The Meadow Pipit well illustrates this; they are ubiquitous in summer, but vacate the fells entirely during the winter months in favour of the coastal plain or southern climes. Possibly the only true resident bird of our mountains is the Raven, that resilient crag-nester remarkable not only for its tolerance of severe climate, but also for its early breeding habits; not infrequently it has completed its clutch of eggs by the beginning of March, when the worst of a Cumbrian winter may still be on its way. They are on occasion quite unjustly persecuted by hill shepherds seeking a scapegoat for a dead lamb, although I must concur with Col. Ryves when he observes in his *Birdlife of Cornwall* that the shy Raven will approach even a carcass with the greatest of caution 'as if it may still be alive'.

It is not unusual for the Raven's crag to be shared by Peregrine, although an uneasy relationship will exist between the two; indeed they appear to antagonise one another constantly and the resultant interaction can be a breathtaking spectacle, for they are both exceedingly agile birds. The Peregrine usually dominates such skirmishes, but not invariably—I have on several occasions witnessed an exasperated falcon half close its wings and dive out of view, closely pursued by its tormentor. Relentlessly persecuted since the late 18th century by gamekeepers, and hounded by egg collectors from the mid-19th century, the Peregrine population survived an official extermination order during the Second World War, tenaciously holding onto a few traditional eyrie sites. The most serious threat, however, was yet to come—a rapid and universal decline in breeding success noticed from the late 1950s, later traced to the presence of toxic pesticide residues in pigeon species, the Peregrine's favoured prey in many areas. Pigeons were contaminated when they fed on grain treated with the chlorinated hydrocarbon insecticides aldrin and dieldrin, at that time in widespread use. Following the withdrawal of these the Peregrine has steadily recovered its pre-war numbers, giving further evidence of its remarkable resilience.

The Buzzard must perhaps be regarded as the third large bird of the crags, although it nests in a variety of habitats and the lower fellside woods are its true stronghold. Despite its relative abundance in the Lakes (an average of 15 pairs breed annually in my own valley alone), many visitors choose to deny its existence and prefer to report sightings of 'Golden Eagle' everywhere. The truth is that we have just two pairs of Eagle breeding in Lakeland at present, plus the odd footloose immature. And, of course, a great many Buzzards.

Golden Eagle (imm.)

Kestrels too are opportunist breeders, utilising a wide variety of habitat, from disused quarries to old crows' nests. It is unusual to see them in the high fells, but they often frequent the lower slopes, where unimproved rough pasture provides ideal country for the voles and mice that form the bulk of a Kestrel's diet.

Feral Pigeon will be noticed on many Lakeland crags, although not, I suspect, on any crag tenanted by *Falco peregrinus*! Jackdaws also warrant inclusion here; these birds very often overrun some of the lower crags, as at Buckbarrow in Wasdale, almost to the exclusion of other species. I know of several abandoned quarries, in particular, which are used solely by large colonies of Jackdaws, both for breeding and roosting.

Fellsides

Around 3000 BC, clearance began of the large tracts of forest that formerly blanketed most of upland Britain. This was initiated by Neolithic man as farming replaced the nomadic hunting and gathering existence of Mesolithic times. Deforestation has continued ever since, aided from about 800 BC onwards by a wetter climate which stimulated bog growth and consequent sphagnum expansion, inhibiting forest regeneration. Despite the depressing efficiency with which we have cleared the fells of indigenous vegetation, and the further denudation inflicted by grazing livestock, there is at least one compensation in land being devoted to sheep farming. By the middle of the last century, land enclosure had become essential and the pattern of dry-stone walls that is so characteristic of Lakeland's landscape today began to emerge. In the mountains, walls were built as boundaries, often along seemingly impossible courses; in the valleys they separated livestock, bordered tracks or were sometimes erected simply to clear fields of stone. Whatever their purpose, dry-stone walls quite unintentionally created a valuable wildlife habitat. The numerous nooks and crannies provide shelter and ideal nesting sites for such birds as Wheatear and Ring Ousel, whilst the relatively rich insect life harboured by walls attract birds like the Pied Wagtail. A survey I conducted one year in Eskdale revealed 12 pairs of nesting wagtails in a 3km section of roadside wall! Unfortunately, the mortality rate of the young birds emerging from nests straight onto the road at its busiest time of year was disastrously high.

Meadow Pipits, as we have previously noted, are abundant in the Lakeland fells in summer. They prefer open sheepwalk country up to about 750m and nest in boulder crevices or among grass tussocks. Their nests are probably those most commonly parasitised by Cuckoos in these parts; a nest found by my dog in the Wasdale fells contained an almost fully fledged Cuckoo which, by opening its bill to reveal a startling vermilion gape, seemed able to requisition food from almost any passing small bird.

Wheatear

Rocky fellsides and stone-walled mountain pastures, in fact anywhere in the fells with good boulder perches, will be inhabited by the Wheatear. It is generally our first mountain migrant to return in spring (the earliest date I have recorded them is March 14th), but most arrive in the first week of April. The arrival of the Wheatear is closely followed by that of the Ring Ousel, a bird mostly confined to regular haunts, especially scree slopes and other types of rough boulder terrain above 300m. It is in the crevices of these stony slopes that Ring Ousels nest and they can prove exceedingly difficult to locate, even when a constant fluty refrain indicates their presence. In common with their lowland counterpart, the Blackbird, they eat mostly grubs and beetles. In autumn, however, their pre-migratory diet includes many berries, particularly bilberries where these are common. Later to arrive are Whinchats, typically encountered delivering their far-reaching song from the top of a low bush, whence they may make short fly-catching sallies, although they mainly feed on beetles and larvae on the ground. Whinchats are not common, yet they appear to be far more adaptable than the resident Stonechat, and make use of quite a wide range of habitat, including bracken, in which to nest. Stonechats tend to occupy areas of gorse and are not well represented in Lakeland, although many can be seen near the coast in winter. Sadly, they do not seem able to survive prolonged cold weather and at the time of writing, the inland population has yet to recover from the severe winter of 1981/2.

Very few birds utilise the extensive bracken cover, although Yellowhammers prefer it to the open fell and an increasing number of Reed Bunting nest in it.

In the high mountains passage birds are scarce. Dotterel must rate as one of the most exciting and can sometimes be seen on the high plateaux in early May, en route for northern breeding grounds. Locations of the few pairs which breed in the Lake District are wisely kept secret. Small flocks of over-wintering Snow Bunting and Twite are commoner than many people suppose, although they also occur on lower ground, especially near the coast. A few Twite linger to breed in the fells, usually on heather moorlands.

Moorlands

Moorland is of quite limited extent in the Lake District; level ground of any kind is scarce in the fells and little of it retains the formerly luxuriant heather growth, encouraged by rotational burning since early Victorian times to provide cover and food for Red Grouse. In many areas sheep have reduced these fine grouse moors to mere patchy growths of heather on the less accessible crag ledges and gullies. This is tragic, since heather moorland is probably the most productive upland bird habitat, especially where crags provide nest sites for birds such as Raven and Peregrine. Some moors remain, however, such as those near Kirkby and Devoke Water, the Shap fells, or north of Skiddaw. Others, like Burnmoor and Hawkshead Moor, survive in name only, and were long ago sacrificed to sheep grazing or afforestation, or more recently 'improved' by marginal land reclamation schemes.

In addition to ling and cross-leaved heather, bilberry and bracken sometimes grow on drier moorland slopes, whilst areas of blanket bog are dominated by cotton grass with mat grass and heath rush. Meadow Pipits again predominate, although some Skylark also breed, not that this unduly perturbs the dashing Merlin, which is partial to both. These tiny falcons are a joy to watch, both when hunting fast and low over the ground, or in spirited pursuit of a lark. Robert Gray has documented the prowess of a Merlin deviously capturing Snipe, and I have myself witnessed some extremely shrewd hunting behaviour, including a co-operative technique involving both male and female birds. For a variety of reasons, the Merlin population is currently declining. Gamekeepers have traditionally meted out the same justice that they applied to the Peregrine, although there is no logic in this, since the Merlin's greatest 'crime' has never been more than the taking of small passerines. Their persecution led the Rev. McPherson to comment in 1892, 'surely future generations will bitterly regret the short-sighted policy at present in fashion'. More recent pressures are only too familiar to conservationists—agricultural chemicals used in the arable wintering areas of Merlins, and the encroachment of moorland forestry.

Another moorland raptor, the Hen Harrier, is predominantly a spring and autumn migrant, although occasionally pairs stay to breed. They prey on a wide variety of species, from voles to Red Grouse, typically quartering the ground at low level in rather delicate gull-like flight, then dropping onto their quarry with tail widely fanned in a neat stalling pirouette.

As well as the now thinly distributed Red Grouse, small numbers of Black

Ring Ouzel

15

Grouse can be found in some localities. They tend to frequent lower moorland and rushy heathland areas, especially along forest edges or in places with a light birch or pine cover, such as that within Grizedale Forest.

A further bird to which reference must be made is to my mind the most remarkable of any found at high altitude. The Wren must occupy virtually every type of habitat in Lakeland, from coastal sand dunes to the rocky plateaux and summits of the highest fells, where it can be quite disconcerting to hear its vigorous, yet melodic warbling in such an incongruous environment.

Red Grouse

Upland Woods
The climax woodland of the Lakeland fells is sessile oakwood, restricted today to a few fragments of the original cover—the Keskadale and Birkrigg Oaks in the Newlands valley being the examples most often quoted. These lie at an altitude of 300 to 500m and support little birdlife because of their exposed position and lack of ground vegetation. Elsewhere grow occasional rowans, whose berries may attract thrushes, or junipers, charcoal from which was much valued by the gunpowder industry.

Upland Afforestation
It is ironic that following our past depredation of upland vegetation, we are now increasingly re-furbishing fell-sides and moorlands with tree cover. The quality of this cover, however, cannot be considered to be anything like that of the original. The afforestation of upland areas with rapid growing species such as Sitka Spruce or Lodgepole Pine causes habitats which have remained static for hundreds of years under a regime of sheep grazing to become suddenly dynamic, and an understanding of the various phases involved in the maturation of a coniferous forest is fundamental to the study of its birds.

The first stage in 'planting up' moorland is to enclose it and so exclude herbivores. Combined with drainage and some nutrient replenishment, this stimulates plant growth, which becomes relatively luxuriant with the young trees as only a small component of the new ecosystem. Meadow Pipits are particularly abundant at this stage due to the increased insect population, whilst Wheatears and Skylarks decline with the demise of short grassland. Rodents thrive, especially voles, and their presence may attract the Short-eared Owl and the Hen Harrier, although these disappear once the young trees begin to exclude access and light from the ground cover. A scrub-like cover is formed, which temporarily encourages warblers such as Willow, Grasshopper and Sedge, Whitethroat and other birds, perhaps including Redpoll and even Nightjar. Time is up, however, for the Meadow Pipits and they depart, along with perching birds like the Whinchat and Stonechat. The thicket becomes denser, favouring only canopy feeders like Goldcrests, Coal Tits and Chaffinches, whilst brashing of the dead lower branches leaves piles of debris valuable for foraging Robins, Wrens and Dunnocks.

At about 15 years old, the forest will accommodate a bird community probably consisting predominantly of Goldcrests, Coal Tits, Chaffinches, Wrens and Treecreepers, with Siskins and possibly other tit and thrush species present. Larger birds may include Woodpigeon, Woodcock, Tawny Owl and Sparrowhawk. More birds will be present when some diversity is afforded within the forest, such as unplanted lacunae of moorland, or a mixture of tree species. Upland predators, such as the Golden Eagle, Merlin and Raven, will all be adversely affected by afforestation. Merlins will often tenaciously hold onto their breeding grounds during this encroachment, sometimes adopting old crows' nests for nesting, but they still need access to open moor to hunt. As a compensation, however, we can expect an increase in Goshawk numbers, fuelled by the loss of falconers' birds and encouraged by the increased coniferous habitat.

Willow Warbler

Dipper

The Forestry Commission's first plantation in the Lake District was at Whinlatter Pass in the north-west, and dates from 1919. Little regard was paid to the amenity value of the area and the forest's structure is one of serried ranks of even-aged trees so deplored by latter-day conservationists. In 1925 and 1926 the Commission acquired most of Ennerdale above the lake and began a similar planting regime, using larch with Norway and Sitka Spruce. At Thirlmere, the results of a more enlightened approach to afforestation can be seen, with mature hardwoods, benefiting from the exclusion of sheep, being allowed to regenerate naturally among the conifers. (*See also* Grizedale Forest.)

Hill Tarns and Mountain Streams

Red Tarn lies east of Helvellyn at an altitude just short of 800 metres and is typical of the many glacial corrie tarns to be found in the Lake District. Their waters are cold and largely sterile, supporting little in the way of birdlife. The tarn outflows are youthful, fast-flowing streams, tumbling over and cutting through acidic rocks and moorland. Aquatic life is sparse and the larvae-eating Dipper requires a large territory in order to sustain itself. Dipper densities in the less acid and relatively fertile water downstream are markedly higher, although still not as high as in comparable areas in the Peak District, where the alkaline rock gives rise to an enriched aquatic insect life. The Dipper occurs at surprising altitudes, albeit in small numbers, but often they will forage in several different headstreams of a high valley, whereas their counterparts in the dales have a linear territory along one river only. Grey Wagtails also feed upon insects found in streams, although they do not venture as far upstream as the Dipper, nor do they have the remarkable abilities of the latter when seeking out food, for the Dipper is competent at swimming, diving and even walking along the stream bed in quite fast-moving water.

Common Sandpipers are breeding visitors encountered on many rivers, although they are scarce on fast flowing fellside streams owing to a lack of shingle beds on which to nest. They occur on quite high altitude tarns too, as at Seathwaite Tarn in the Duddon Valley, perhaps favoured because of its shallow edges. We expect 'Summer Snipe', as they are sometimes named, from the second week in April onwards; departure coastwards usually occurs in early July.

A recent colonist of moorland becks is the Goosander, in spring regularly seen commuting downstream from their streamside nest holes to richer feeding waters. Their flight is fast and determined, following every twist and turn of the river. In winter, they are more commonly seen on the larger hill tarns and on some lakes, often in the company of Red-breasted Mergansers. Current research suggests that male Goosanders migrate northward in June/July to moult and return in September, but I am not aware of any recoveries of ringed Lakeland birds to support this thesis.

Hill tarns of less elevation than Red Tarn vary greatly in character. Unlike corrie tarns, many are quite productive and attractive to waterfowl, although not to the same extent as the fertile lowland lakes. Some, such as Eel Tarn, Eskdale, have marginal vegetation which provides nesting cover for Little Grebes, Coot and Snipe, whilst others, such as Devoke Water, are stocked with fish, which may be exploited by the sawbills or Grey Heron. It is in winter, however, that tarns become especially significant habitats, particularly during inclement weather, when they may temporarily host storm-driven seaduck and divers. Most familiar of the wintering duck are Goldeneye, whose distinctive peaked-head outline is unmistakable even as a distant silhouette. Pochards, too, are quite regular winter visitors; one March I surprised a group of six on Low Tarn in Wasdale at an altitude of nearly 600m. The tarn was 90% frozen over, and near-blizzard conditions prevailed. Mute Swans are rare on any but lowland waters, yet I have known both Whooper and the less common Bewick's Swan to visit hill tarns.

Reference must also be made here to the Black-headed Gull, which will readily form quite large breeding colonies in the fells, particularly on tarns with small islands where their nests have a better chance of remaining unmolested by predators such as the fox. These colonies typically have a non-breeding component roosting nearby, the majority feeding in the valley fields during the day. Over the years, the gulls' droppings may gradually enrich the sterile peat surrounding the colony, giving rise to communities of richer plant and insect life.

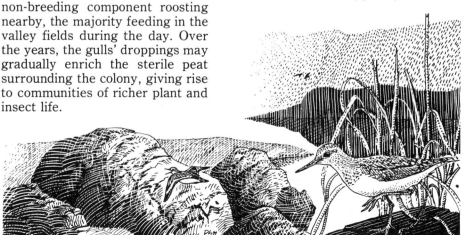

Common Sandpipers

WOODLAND

As we have already noted, little remains of the original sessile oakwood cover and most present-day woodlands, comprising oak, birch, alder, ash, hazel, rowan and perhaps holly, owe their existence to the bygone industries which exploited them. Many were managed for centuries as enclosed coppice, but now grow wild, forming the pleasant semi-natural woodland so typical of the Lakeland scene. They are often devoid of a shrub layer unless fenced from sheep and deer, but bracken proliferates, especially in the well-drained woods clinging to rocky, boulder-strewn slopes. Where grazing is light, daffodils, primroses, wood anemones and bluebells may grow. Woodland of this kind can be found in most dales; good examples are Naddle Forest in Mardale, Scales Wood near Buttermere, Baysbrown Wood in Great Langdale, Glencoyne and Hallin Fell woods near Ullswater, Low Wood on the shores of Brothers Water and the woods of Longsleddale. The most extensive coppice woods, however, were in the High Furness area, between Windermere and the Duddon Valley, where woodland provided the economic foundation of southern Lakeland from the middle ages onward. Timber from these woods was used for housing, boats, domestic and agricultural equipment of all kinds, bobbins, barrels, hoops and swills, and also provided charcoal for iron ore furnaces into the 20th century. Coppice woodlands were therefore quite valuable and a very profitable way of utilising ground too rugged for agriculture. Unfortunately many are now doomed, due to lack of regeneration caused by grazing livestock.

Oak Woods

Woods dominated by the sessile oak are characterised by three particular birds, all of which are summer migrants; the Pied Flycatcher, Wood Warbler and Redstart. Of the three, the Wood Warbler is the most localised, although fears of a decline, first noted in 1960, appear not to have been realised. Like the Willow Warbler, it builds a domed nest within a hollow of the ground. Pied Flycatchers commonly nest some 2—3m from the ground in the crevices of mature trees, although in woods without these natural cavities they will readily take to nest boxes. My YOC group in Eskdale had encouraging success with a nest box scheme in a plantation predominantly of larch, which has few natural nest holes. We found that flycatchers had a noticeable preference for boxes sited near the woodland margin or in clearings, presumably because this made aerial

Pied Flycatcher

feeding sorties easier. Similarly, Redstarts will use boxes of the open-fronted design, although shortage of nest sites is not generally a great problem for them as they often take advantage of crevices in buildings and walls. The name 'Redstart', incidentally, derives from 'Red-stoert', meaning red tail, a feature of plumage common to both sexes. Associated with oak woodland is the Tree Pipit, another summer visitor and one usually found where the trees are more scattered, such as the upper margins of woods; Tree Pipits are ground-nesters, but require suitable song perches from which to commence their aerial display flight. Two other species which rate highly in oakwoods are the Blue and Great Tit; the former has an especial affinity to oak and, like the Coal Tit, feeds high in the canopy. Willow Tits are not common; they excavate their own nests in rotten timber and so require the presence of old or soft-timbered trees. In the Lake District they tend to be confined to areas of birch and alder. A recent trend is the increase in numbers of Long-tailed Tit, especially in young coppices, or those with a more developed understorey. Of the other birds, Chaffinch, Wren, Robin, Carrion Crow, Woodpigeon and Starling are common in oak woods as they are in most woodland types. Warblers, however, seem to be poorly represented, excepting Willow and Wood Warbler; perhaps this is because of the absence of a good shrub layer.

Alder Woods

Alder forms an important element of many Lakeland oakwoods, but is more noticeable as a river and lakeside tree. In winter it often attracts groups of Siskin and Redpoll which feed from the tiny cones.

Birch Woods

The upper fringes of sessile oakwoods frequently grade into birch woodland, which is often in a state of semi-decay owing to lack of regeneration and the relatively short life-span of birch trees. Fungi and wood-boring insects are therefore abundant; the latter are commonly exploited by Great Spotted Woodpecker, which finds nest excavation in the soft timber of birch easier than in the trunks of sessile oak. In spring the dominant bird is the Willow Warbler, with a high occurrence of Chaffinches, Tree Pipits, Wrens and Robins.

Ash and Hazel Woods

The mountain limestone of south Lakeland, which outcrops at Yewbarrow, Whitbarrow and Underbarrow, provides a rich soil upon which woods of ash, hazel, elm, oak and lime flourish. Because of the structure of these woods, far more light is admitted to the understorey than in an oak-dominated wood, so that a comparatively luxuriant shrub-layer can develop. This generally comprises rowan, bird cherry, hawthorn, blackthorn and whitebeam, a combination attractive to Whitethroats and Garden Warblers among others. Small numbers of Marsh Tits occur here, although other tit species are not abundant, perhaps reflecting the less prolific insect life of ash-hazel woodland.

21

Other Woodlands

During the 17th and 18th centuries it became fashionable for private landowners to plant both native and alien tree species in the estates surrounding halls, castles and other prestigious residences. Good examples of these 'amenity woodlands' can be seen at Muncaster Castle, Duddon Hall, Graythwaite Woods and elsewhere throughout the Lake District, particularly in the Windermere-Rydal-Grasmere valley. They were initially developed from down-graded woodland or old coppice; pine was one of the first trees to be added, and larch, beech and sycamore were introduced later, often underplanted with rhododendron. Scots Pine is now well naturalised, having spread by seeding to occupy the thin soils of rocky knolls. It is of especial significance to the Crossbill, a very localised breeding bird whose numbers seem directly related to the pine's seed crop. The Crossbill population is sometimes augmented in autumn by parties of visiting continental birds. Other notable birds of the pine are Siskins, Goldcrests and Coal Tits.

Although not as rich as oak, beech woods support a large invertebrate community and this helps to compensate for the lack of a developed shrub and field layer resulting from the small amount of daylight admitted by the canopy. The commonest birds are usually Chaffinches and Blackbirds, followed by Great Tits, Wrens and Robins. Woodpigeons often adopt beech tops as roosts, whilst Green Woodpeckers and Jays favour the open type of woodland that beech tends to form. Summer visitors generally include Willow Warblers, Chiffchaffs, Redstarts, Wood Warblers and occasional Blackcaps.

Grizedale Forest

In its most recent forest at Grizedale, the Forestry Commission has pursued a policy of multiple-use management with a much higher regard for wildlife conservation and recreation. Native oakwoods have been preserved for hardwood timber production, whilst areas of degraded sheepwalk have been planted with larch, spruce and pine. Only the higher pastures, such as those between Grizedale and Coniston Water, sustain dense blocks of conifers, leaving the richer valley land for farming. The upland area is now an important haven for red and roe deer, fox, badger and red squirrel, as well as for many species of bird. Small numbers of Black Grouse also occur, an otherwise scarce bird in the Lake District; and in the early 1970s an unsuccessful attempt was made to re-introduce Capercaillie. The Forestry Commission is keen to stress the amenity value of the area; at Satterthwaite there is an informative museum and wildlife centre, and numerous nature trails have been provided, plus some observation towers and photographic hides which give more intimate views of wildlife. A nest box scheme has boosted the numbers of smaller birds, in particular Pied Flycatchers and Redstarts, both unusual species in commercial forests.

Other Woodland Birds

Although never encountered in large numbers, the Spotted Flycatcher is present in most deciduous woods where flying insects are plentiful. Open woods, parkland and orchards are its preferred habitat, a preference shared by the few Lesser Spotted Woodpeckers in the Lake District. Cumbria is near the northern limit of occurrence of these diminutive woodpeckers—a bird best looked for in the mature alders of south Lakeland. Easily overlooked, Treecreepers may be found exploring the trunks of a wide variety of trees through Lakeland. That other bark-gymnast, the Nuthatch, appears to be fast colonising oak and other Cumbrian woods. R. H. Brown in *Lakeland Birds* records only one sighting in 50 years of Lakeland bird-watching, but since my first observations of individuals in central Lakeland during the early 1970s, Nuthatch have become an increasingly familiar sight in all types of deciduous woodland and pairs are now established even in the remote western dales.

Hawfinch are shy and elusive birds of mature mixed woodland. Although scarce, their quiet nature and tendency to nest high may have led us to under-record them. They are particularly partial to the kernels of cherry, damson, sloe or hawthorn and these are the best woodlands in which to seek them.

Locally within woodlands, hollows of poorly drained soil occur, at best supporting a few birch trees, but more often forming damp sedge and sphagnum-carpeted clearings, attractive to winter Woodcock. In spring, these birds generally choose to nest among the bracken and forest undergrowth, where their superb disruptive camouflage can be used to full advantage.

Buzzard are common in the mixed wood and field habitat of the dales. They are sedentary and have well-defined territories, usually containing three or four nests, often all in the same species of tree. The final selection of nest in any one year seems to be an almost last-minute affair, all the nests having been

previously decorated with bright sprigs of larch or even pieces of orange baler twine!

Another well distributed woodland raptor is the Sparrowhawk, a bird more regularly seen hunting along hedgerows, or soaring over woods and fell in spring, than in its woodland haunts, where the discovery of a plucking post may be the only indication of this secretive bird's presence.

Finally, we come to the Tawny Owl, a resident of many types of woodland, from isolated old oaks to quite dense, but generally deciduous, forest. One conifer that is patronised, however, is the pine, which is tall and has sturdy lateral branches for daytime roosting. If it is discovered in this position by smaller birds, the owl will be mobbed unmercifully and the accompanying noise is a good clue as to an owl's whereabouts. Once located, Tawny Owls are easy to approach in daylight; often they merely press themselves against the main trunk and close their conspicuous eyes to narrow slits.

LAKES AND RIVERS

Lakeland's waters and meres are extremely diverse bird habitats. They also vary considerably in character, partly because they reflect the underlying geology of the district, but also because the deposition of silt and spread of aquatic and lake-edge vegetation has not been uniform, being dependent upon the nature and extent of the inflowing drainage. This has created a spectrum of productivity, from the little altered 'primitive' lakes with rocky shores and clear waters, sustaining few plants and animals, to extensively modified lakes rich in nutrients, which support relatively rich aquatic life.

Wastwater, Ennerdale Water and Buttermere are all 'primitive' lakes. Their acid waters are not normally attractive to birdlife and numbers even of common birds, such as Mallard, are low. A few fish-eating species, however, benefit from the unclouded water which enables them to see their prey clearly. Red-breasted Merganser and Goosander are two good examples; co-incidentally, both are quite recent colonists of the Lake District. Mergansers rapidly spread from a breeding nucleus at Ravenglass during the early 1950s. They first bred on Windermere in 1957; by 1968, 110 adults were present, and in that year 138 young were raised! Goosanders expanded their range more recently, most noticeably from around 1970.

The remaining lakes fit into a scale of productivity culminating with such lakes as Ullswater, Windermere and Esthwaite Water. Many birds are wholly reliant on these lakes for food, sanctuary and nest sites, the most aquatic being Little and Great Crested Grebes, which feed mostly on small fish and large invertebrates, and rarely leave the water. They construct semi-floating nests anchored to emergent vegetation and Great Crested Grebes in particular tend to be confined to lakes with reedy fringes. Tufted Duck and Pochard are diving duck, occupying very similar niches, yet they avoid competition by feeding selectively, the former preying predominantly upon invertebrates, whilst Pochard depend more on aquatic plant food. Both are scarce breeders in the Lake District and are very much more apparent in winter. Exclusively vegetarian, Coot either dive for submerged plant food, or pluck it from the lake edge. They breed on most lakes and many tarns, building substantial semi-floating nests capable of adjusting to varying water levels. Moorhens are not quite as widespread, favouring quieter stretches of river or lakeside where dense vegetation provides cover. Pairs of Mute Swan are resident on most lowland waters with up to seven pairs breeding on Windermere; but as in other parts of the country, lead poisoning and discarded fishing lines are taking their toll.

Greylag Geese are a familiar sight on many lakes, yet their re-establishment as a breeding species is comparatively recent. Greylag eggs of Scottish origin were hatched out at a small private reserve near the Duddon estuary in 1961 and successive years by Jim Ellwood of the South Cumberland Wildfowlers' Association. Stock was introduced at several locations to establish nuclei throughout the Lake District and since the first reported nesting in the wild at Coniston in 1963 the geese have colonised most of the suitable lakes. Canada Geese were not introduced into Cumbria until the late 1950s, but many flocks

Goosanders

can now be seen, such as those at Killington Reservoir and at Haweswater, where 160 geese have been recorded.

Of the dabbling duck, Mallards are both widespread and common, although Red-breasted Mergansers now outnumber them as a breeding species on some lakes. Teal are widely scattered, but sparse breeders; their highest numbers occur in autumn on the more sheltered lakes.

Dependent to a lesser extent on lake habitats is the Grey Heron, frequently to be seen stalking fish in the shallow lake margins. They can equally well find food such as frogs and eels, their favourite prey, in ditches and damp meadows. Sedge Warblers and Reed Buntings, too, are by no means exclusively confined to lake edge vegetation, although the extensive fens at the head of such lakes as Bassenthwaite and Esthwaite are ideal haunts. Thinly distributed and rarely encountered these days is the Kingfisher, formerly a regular bird of most lowland lakes and rivers. Kingfishers are especially susceptible to hard winters, yet this alone does not explain their decline, as numbers recovered well after the 1962/3 winter. Except for the Common Sandpiper, eight pairs of which once bred within a 7km stretch of Ullswater shoreline, few waders breed by the water's edge. Redshank, Oystercatcher, Dunlin and Lapwing occasionally nest close to lakes, however, usually on marshy fields.

The omnipresent midges that make lakeside camping such a trial in summer, attract Swifts, Swallows, House and Sand Martins. Of these only the Sand Martin generally nests near water.

Visits from non-breeding Herring, Great and Lesser Black-backed Gulls are commonplace in summer and there is a regular passage of Lesser Black-backed through the Lake District in August and September, when the major lakes are used for roosting and feeding. Post-breeding dispersal of inland Black-headed Gull colonies builds up quite large roosts on larger lakes and their numbers are further augmented by the arrival of continental birds.

On the lowland rivers, Dippers and Grey Wagtails are common, nesting among tree roots or in the crevices of stone bridges. Often their presence is betrayed by tell-tale white uric acid deposits on favourite mid-river perching stones. Both species tend to migrate downstream in cold weather, often to lakes or the coast, although many Grey Wagtails move south for the winter months.

The Lakes in Winter

The numbers and diversity of duck on the lakes vary with the severity of the weather. Rough weather can bring many visitors to the relatively sheltered waters inland and this makes winter the most rewarding time for observing waterfowl. Populations of the resident dabbling duck, Mallard and Teal, are greatly swollen by the arrival of birds from the north, especially on Bassenthwaite and Windermere, where over 1,000 Mallard have been recorded. In autumn particularly, many Mallard and Teal roost during the day on lakes, and move out at dusk to feed on adjacent farmland, free from agricultural and other disturbance. They therefore tend to favour lakes such as Bassenthwaite, which are surrounded by arable land. These lakes also offer more shelter, as they are low-lying and have shallow shores with many bays and headlands.

By contrast, large numbers of gulls, notably Black-headed, Herring and Common, feed in the fields during daylight and roost on lakes at night. Like the duck, they bring back considerable quantities of nutrients which are deposited in the lakes via their droppings. Large winter gull roosts occur on Bassenthwaite, Haweswater and Ullswater, where counts have estimated between 15,000 and 20,000 gulls, predominantly Common. In most years these wintering flocks have left by mid-April, but small groups may linger until June.

Coot nesting on the higher tarns gather on lowland waters in winter, where they are joined by visiting birds. 850 Coot were recorded on Windermere one February and the totals of 350 on Derwentwater and 210 on Ullswater are not untypical.

Present throughout the year on some lakes, Cormorants are most often seen in winter. Up to 48 birds have roosted at Haweswater, with further groups on most central and eastern lakes, where they often roost in trees by the water's edge and on islands.

Wigeon are the most numerous duck in winter, when most are found on or near the coast, but flocks also occur inland; Bassenthwaite and Ullswater are good locations, as are some smaller waters, such as Bigland Tarn near Newby Bridge and Whin's Pond near Penrith. Pintail are less common visitors to the lakes, and only occasional single ones are seen.

Of the diving duck, Pochard and Tufted Duck reach modest numbers on many lakes, notably Bassenthwaite and Derwentwater. Goldeneye are one of the most characteristic winter diving duck, arriving from mid-October onwards and inhabiting lakes, tarns and rivers until late April. Up to 300 birds, mainly

Greylag Geese/Ennerdale

females, may be present on Windermere, the third most important wintering site for Goldeneye in England. Elsewhere, maximum numbers generally occur in spring, prior to departure. Increasingly, stragglers tend to remain into May and some over-summer, indicating that breeding is likely in the near future.

Many lakes, among them Bassenthwaite and Windermere, lie conspicuously on regular goose migration routes; yet the geese seldom alight, except perhaps for an occasional individual decoyed by the resident Greylags. Both Whooper and the scarcer Bewick's Swan visit the lakes. Numbers fluctuate greatly from winter to winter, but are generally low, and many parties consist merely of a family group. The largest flocks have been seen on Derwentwater and Bassenthwaite Lake; smaller groups are liable to turn up on any of the lakes, and many tarns also, including Yewtree, Blelham and Loughrigg.

Three species of diver occur sporadically during hard weather; Red-throated are the most regularly seen, particularly on Windermere, Coniston Water and Ullswater, and many are found ailing or dead. Most inland Great Northern Diver records relate to Windermere, but I have noted occasional birds on Ullswater and Wastwater. Black-throated Divers have been seen on several small waters, such as Loughrigg Tarn, Devoke Water and Killington Reservoir, yet on comparatively few of the larger lakes, again with the exception of Windermere.

Several other rare birds may turn up after a protracted period of severe weather. These birds are, of course, impossible to predict, but regular and systematic observation of any lake or lowland tarn in winter should be rewarding. The three rarer grebes, Red-necked, Black-necked and Slavonian, are all annually reported; the Slavonian is the one most commonly recorded inland. Scaup, Long-tailed Duck, Common Scoter and Smew are also possibilities.

Goldeneyes

Enclosure, drainage and other land 'improvement' schemes have robbed the dales of the swampy alder and willow carr that formerly dominated them. Most valley land now comprises improved grazing pasture and fields of standard hay grasses.

Farmland

Lakeland valleys have few hedgerows, an important component of arable habitats elsewhere. Land enclosure has been accomplished by dry-stone walls, the crevices and cavities of which, we have already noted, provide many birds with shelter, food and nest sites. In the dales these are likely to be Pied Wagtail, Redstart and Wren. Around the periphery of the Lake District the familiar agricultural pattern of field and hedgerow asserts itself; it is here that we find the majority of Partridge, Lapwing, Woodpigeon and Corn Bunting, or perhaps glimpse a Sparrowhawk hunting low alongside a hedge and pouncing with characteristic panache upon its oblivious quarry on the other side. In winter, Redwing and Fieldfare join the foraging Rook and Jackdaw on open fields. Some of the best areas for birds are the patches of unkempt land one occasionally finds in the corners of fields, perhaps overrun with thistle and weed. Sadly, these areas are fast disappearing as farmers attempt to maximise productivity.

Meadows, Mires and Mosses

Also largely lost are the dale meadows, although a few linger on in most valleys. These are the special haunt of Yellow Wagtails. The unimproved, poorly drained pasture found in many valleys and surrounding some lakes forms stretches of mire, supporting a vegetation of tall reeds and sedges interspersed with alder and willow scrub. These are inhabited by Snipe and from October to February by the visiting Jack Snipe. Where the reeds are extensive, Sedge and Grasshopper Warblers may breed, although neither is conspicuous and both are best detected by their song. Other birds of these mire 'fens' include Pheasant and the scarcer Water Rail.

It is appropriate to mention here the very special moss habitats located on raised bog areas surrounding the Morecambe Bay estuaries. These brackish swamps and reed fen became increasingly acidic as they built up, eventually forming sphagnum peat. The cutting of this peat and

Bittern

Snipe

improvement in agricultural drainage locally has radically altered them and many, such as Rusland Moss, have been colonised by pine and birch and these are good areas in which to look for Nightjars.

Heathwaite Moss on the Duddon estuary and Holker Moss on the Leven are wetter bogs not yet affected by the lowering of the water table. Many mosses are valuable bird habitats in much the same way as valley mires, but some are exceptional, being both extensive and diverse. The finest of these, Leighton Moss, where Bitterns breed, is now managed by the Royal Society for the Protection of Birds.

Buildings and Gardens

Buildings are a noteworthy artificial habitat; House Martins nest under eaves, Swallows occupy nests in the beams and rafters of barns, and Swifts breed in some of the larger villages. The many derelict barns and farm outbuildings are traditional roosting and breeding haunts of Barn Owls, although renovation of these for holiday homes has adversely affected owl numbers. This has been alleviated to some extent by stricter planning control.

In farmyards, spilt grain attracts finches, sparrows and Starlings, whilst silage pits are a haven for Pied and Grey Wagtails. Here, as in other parts of the country, food is provided on window ledges and bird tables throughout winter. Many of the birds enticed by this bonus would be alien to suburban gardens, however; Great Spotted Woodpecker, Redpoll and Siskin may be quite regular visitors, in addition to the usual Blue, Great and Coal Tit, Chaffinch and Greenfinch. In Eskdale, a December Blackcap once joined them and red squirrels are not unknown guests. All are ever-vigilant for Sparrowhawks, who well know what oases these feeding stations can be for small birds in a harsh climate.

30

THE COAST

The Cumbrian coast is extensive and diverse, stretching from the great marshes of the Inner Solway southwards to the vast intertidal areas of Morecambe Bay, both regions of exceptional importance to wildfowl and waders. The coastline between them largely consists of a narrow shingle beach with a mixture of sand, shingle and rock below the high water mark; the only major features interrupting this are the Duddon and Esk estuaries and the rocky outcrop of St Bees Head. Perhaps the best way to appreciate this scenery is to travel by train from Lancaster across the Morecambe Bay estuaries to Barrow-in-Furness, and then northwards on the West Cumbria Line to Carlisle.

The South Solway is given only brief attention here, since it is rather distant from the national park, and cannot really be considered in isolation, as there is much interchange of birdlife with the Galloway and Dumfries coast of the firth.

Estuaries

Estuaries are unusual bird habitats in that they support only a small population of breeding birds, yet the number of migrant and over-wintering birds that use them is enormous. The main attraction for these visiting birds is the abundant supply of invertebrate food contained in the rich estuarine mud. One of the few breeding habitats found within the intertidal zone is the saltmarsh, although regular flooding discourages most birds from nesting. A notable exception is the Redshank, whose chicks are able to float during flood periods; in addition, Redshank nests tend to be situated along creek-edges, where the ground is

Shelducks

31

often raised slightly above the surrounding marsh. Oystercatchers, Black-headed Gulls and Common Terns may nest upon marshes that flood only irregularly, whilst the higher saltmarsh, which is frequently grazed by sheep, offers nest sites for Skylark, Meadow Pipit, Linnet and perhaps Lapwing. Immediately above the intertidal area a transitional zone of reedbed and brackish marsh often occurs, such as that around Eskholme Marsh on the River Esk. This can be attractive to species such as Moorhen, Sedge Warbler and Reed Bunting, whilst outside the breeding season they may be the haunt of Teal, or 'freshwater waders' such as Spotted Redshank, Greenshank or Green and Wood Sandpipers.

Although many Shelduck are to be seen on the marshes, they differ from the other birds that use this habitat in that they mostly nest elsewhere and use the intertidal areas merely to raise their young.

Throughout the year, the commonest waders on most Cumbrian estuaries are Curlew, Redshank, Dunlin and Oystercatcher, all of which feed primarily on the mud-flats. The occurrence of other types of estuarine habitat may alter this locally; in winter, for instance, Sanderling may be numerous on areas of sandy shore, whilst Purple Sandpipers and Turnstones will probably dominate rocky outcrops and mussel beds.

In spring the intertidal areas briefly host many species of wader moving north to their breeding grounds, although the return migration in late summer and autumn is the time when peak numbers are generally recorded and the birds seem more inclined to linger. Regular passage waders seen on Cumbrian estuaries include Grey Plover, Curlew Sandpiper, Ruff, Black-tailed Godwit, Whimbrel, Spotted Redshank and Green Sandpiper. In addition, numbers of some waders build up throughout autumn to reach maximum levels in mid-winter. Perhaps the most notable waders that over-winter in large flocks are Oystercatchers, Knot, Dunlin and Curlew.

The waders are an extremely diverse group of birds and differences in the characteristics of bills and legs, in particular, enable them to specialise in their feeding techniques; the short-legged Dunlin and Knot, for example, feed on small crustaceans at the water's edge, whilst godwits, Curlew and Redshank wade out to feed on larger prey, such as lugworms and bivalve molluscs. When the flats are covered by the tide, the waders, prevented from further feeding, retire to their favoured roosts, usually either on the saltmarsh or in nearby fields, and these high-tide congregations generally afford the best opportunities for close observation. Wildfowl, however, such as Greylag

Bar-tailed Godwits

32

Geese, Mallard and Wigeon, feed on the saltmarsh and surrounding agricultural areas, where they are sometimes accompanied by Golden Plover and Lapwing, and then may roost out on the estuary, either afloat or on exposed sandbanks.

Gulls, too, are important estuarine birds, and huge numbers of them breed near to many Cumbrian estuaries. Some, such as the Great Black-backed, Lesser Black-backed and Herring, feed on the intertidal mud and mussel banks, roosting with the waders on the saltmarsh at high tide, whilst others, notably the Black-headed and Common Gulls, feed inland and roost on the intertidal areas at night. Herring Gulls, in particular, are partial to scavenging on local rubbish tips, as at South Walney, for example.

Few species of gulls are strictly resident, the most markedly migrant being the Lesser Black-backed, and although increasing numbers are overwintering in Cumbria, most leave at the end of summer for Southern Europe and North Africa. Populations of the other gulls are augmented by winter visitors, with the highest numbers generally occurring on passage in July and August, with a smaller peak in March on the return migration; the most notable movements are those of Black-headed and Common Gulls.

As well as the seasonal changes in estuarine birdlife, there are less predictable movements of birds caused by severe weather. In winter, large influxes of wildfowl and waders can occur if the freshwater wetland habitats freeze over.

Considering the vast numbers of birds often present on estuaries, it is not surprising that they are favourite haunts for some birds of prey. Peregrine, in particular, are regular winter visitors, mostly preying upon small to medium-sized waders such as Redshank, whilst the Merlin pursues Meadow Pipits, Skylarks, Linnets and other saltmarsh passerines. Wintering Hen Harriers and Short-eared Owls tend to hunt over denser vegetation, like the areas of reed fen behind some saltmarshes. Good locations to look for these exciting birds are the mosses around Morecambe Bay and at Angerton Moss on the Duddon Estuary.

Ringed Plovers

33

Sand Dunes

Open, unstable dune systems with little vegetation cover attract only a limited number of breeding species; there is more diversity on dunes that are consolidated by grassland and scrub. Most species of gull and tern will nest on open dunes, especially the less accessible ones, and some form huge colonies, such as the Black-headed Gulls at Drigg and the Lesser Black-backed and Herring Gulls at South Walney. Of the non-colonial nesting birds, Skylark are by far the commonest, and Shelduck and Red-breasted Merganser perhaps the most interesting; the latter bred for the first time in Cumbria on Drigg Dunes in the early 1950s. Another 'recent' colonist, this time of the dunes at South Walney, is the Eider, which first bred there in 1949 and has since increased in number to a breeding population of over 500 pairs.

Winter is a relatively poor time of year for duneland birds, although occasional groups of Lapwing, Golden Plover, Curlew and gulls may be seen. In spring and autumn, however, many passerine migrants use the dunes; Wheatear and Whinchat are typical of the open areas, whilst the food and shelter provided by the dune scrub attracts large numbers of thrushes and warblers, especially in autumn when the former may feed heavily on the berries of shrubs such as Sea Buckthorn.

Shingle Beaches

Shingle beaches fringe much of the Cumbrian coast. They are the main breeding habitat of Ringed Plover and Little Tern, colonies of the latter often nesting immediately above the high water mark. Oystercatchers and Arctic Tern may also breed on the shingle, but they have much broader habitat tolerances and occupy other coastal habitats as well. Many beaches suffer from human disturbance; a factor which may explain the decline in Little Tern numbers. The vegetated shingle higher up the beach may support Skylarks, Meadow and Rock Pipits and Linnet, whilst in winter diligent searching may reveal Twite or Snow Buntings.

Rocky Coasts

St Bees Head is the only seabird cliff on the Cumbrian coast and features in the second section of this book as the only example of a strictly non-estuarine coastline. Of special interest on cliffs such as St Bees is the preference exhibited by some birds for particular nest sites. A general pattern of bird distribution is noticeable, ranging from Razorbills nesting on the sheltered

Arctic Skua & Common Scoters

lower ledges, through to Fulmars and Herring Gulls on grassy ledges near the cliff top. The middle reaches are inhabited by Kittiwake, which cement their nests to narrow rock ledges using a mixture of algae and guano, and Guillemots, nesting in very high densities on the wider ledges.

Many 'land birds' also commonly breed on sea cliffs, including Kestrel, Stock Dove, Rock Pipit, Starling, Wren and Jackdaw, whilst the cliff-top scrub may hold Dunnock, Stonechat and Linnet.

Outside the breeding season, the cliff face will be generally quiet, although large numbers of some seabirds, in particular Fulmars and Guillemots, sometimes visit the ledges during a spell of fine weather.

Smaller, more broken cliffs occur in some places, such as between Whitehaven and Workington, for example, and these low-profile rocky coasts, although not good breeding habitats, support a variety of winter waders, most notably Purple Sandpipers and Turnstones. Rocky outcrops near the estuaries, like the limestone peninsula at Humphrey Head, are often adopted as high tide roosts by waders feeding on the intertidal area.

Coastal Waters

Inshore waters are important feeding areas for many breeding birds, especially gulls and terns, although others, such as Guillemots and Razorbills, move further offshore to feed.

Outside the breeding season, large seabird passages can occur; those of Fulmar, Manx Shearwater, Gannet, gulls and auks are the most notable. These movements are best observed from headlands or other places where the coastline forms a projecting angle, such as at South Walney. Careful monitoring of seabird passages, or 'seawatching', often reveals less usual birds, such as divers, the rarer species of shearwater, and skuas.

During winter, birds commonly seen feeding offshore include Red-throated Diver, Cormorant, Eider, Common Scoter, Red-breasted Merganser and the ubiquitous Black-headed, Common and Herring Gulls. Certain offshore localities, for example Moricambe Bay on the Solway, are favoured by Scaup, whilst others may attract numbers of Goldeneye.

Sewage outfalls and effluent discharge points often cause concentrations of wintering seabirds because they enrich the invertebrate fauna of the water locally. Other artificial attractions for marine birds are harbours where fish are landed, such as Whitehaven and Workington, which have large numbers of gulls, sometimes including Glaucous and Iceland Gull, and docks, such as Cavendish Dock in Barrow, the relatively warm waters of which benefit many birds, especially grebes and mergansers.

Glaucous Gull (imm.)

SOME BIRDING LOCALITIES

The 20 or so locations in the following section are suggestions, based upon my own birdwatching experience, of places where you can see the main habitat categories described in the first part of this book. Few areas fit neatly into one category and so a generalised classification has been adopted. The selection of sites was extremely difficult; several that I longed to include were just too sensitive, or they had inadequate access or no footpaths. I tend to avoid popular places, but of these some, such as White Moss Common, are very good for birds, even in the height of the holiday season, and so warrant inclusion. The maps are *not* intended to be nature trails. Some indicate routes which link interesting bird-habitats, but many merely recommend areas for further exploration, or good observation points. The relevant map is therefore strongly recommended; the emphasis here is on birds, not on route-finding!

Greenshank

SOME BIRDING LOCALITIES

Key to Numbered Sites

1. Bassenthwaite Lake
2. Borrowdale
3. Brothers Water and Dovedale
4. Longsleddale
5. White Moss Common and Rydal Water
6. Tilberthwaite
7. Brockhole
8. Claife Heights
9. Whitbarrow Scar
10. Morecambe Bay
11. South Walney
12. Duddon Estuary and Angerton Moss
13. Hodbarrow
14. Ravenglass
15. Dalegarth Woods/Devoke Water
16. St Bees Head/Longlands

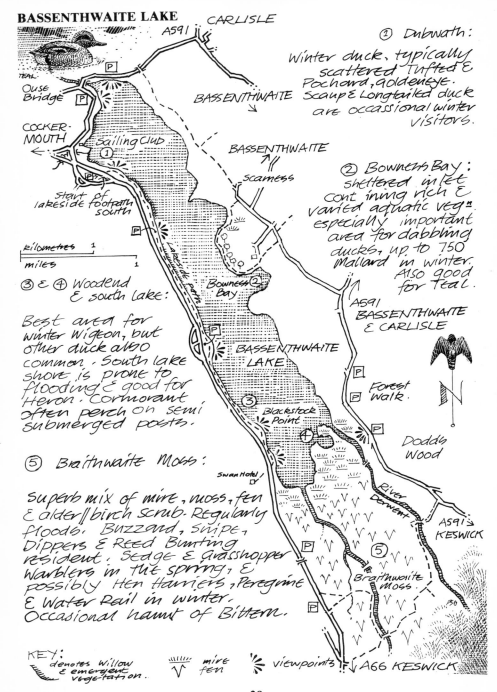

BASSENTHWAITE LAKE

CARLISLE

A591

TEAL

Ouse Bridge

COCKER-MOUTH

Sailing Club ①

start of lakeside footpath south

BASSENTHWAITE

BASSENTHWAITE

Scarness

Lakeside path

Bowness Bay ②

BASSENTHWAITE LAKE

A591
BASSENTHWAITE & CARLISLE

N

Forest Walk.

Dodd's Wood

Blackstock Point ③

④

Swan Hotel

River Derwent

A591 KESWICK

⑤ Braithwaite Moss.

30

① Dubwath:
Winter duck, typically scattered Tufted & Pochard, goldeneye. Scaup & Longtailed duck are occasional winter visitors.

② Bowness Bay:
sheltered inlet cont'ining rich & varied aquatic veg^n especially important area for dabbling ducks, up to 750 Mallard in winter. Also good for teal.

③ & ④ Woodend & south lake:

Best area for winter Wigeon, but other duck also common. South lake shore is prone to flooding & good for Heron. Cormorant often perch on semi submerged posts.

⑤ Braithwaite Moss:

Superb mix of mire, moss, fen & alder//birch scrub. Regularly floods. Buzzard, Snipe, Dippers & Reed Bunting resident. Sedge & Grasshopper Warblers in the spring, & possibly Hen Harriers, Peregrine & Water Rail in winter. Occasional haunt of Bittern.

kilometres 1
miles 1

KEY:
∼∼∼ denotes willow & emergent vegetation.

⌄ mire fen

∖∖ viewpoints

38

① BASSENTHWAITE LAKE   Lake and Mire

OS 1:25,000 NW Sheet/Bartholomew Lake District Map or National Sheet 34

Access: By car—A591 or A66 NE from Keswick.

Bus—Cumberland Motor Services routes 34 and 35 Whitehaven-Cockermouth-Keswick, or route 71 Wigton-Keswick.

Bassenthwaite is the fourth largest of the lakes and one of the most important for waterfowl. More than 70 species of bird breed around the lake, but it is best visited in winter when over 2000 duck may be present. Constant fluctuations in the water level, resulting from the combination of the lake's shallow nature and its large catchment area, have produced long stretches of emergent vegetation and scrub. To the south lies one of the very few areas of extensive mire and reed fen in Lakeland, little disturbed owing to the limited public access. Along the west shore, slightly marred by its proximity to the A66, a footpath from Dubwath to beyond Blackstock Point affords excellent views of the whole lake. The pleasant bays and promontories of the east shore are best sampled at Bowness Bay, walking north to Scarness. Dinghy sailing, largely confined to the northern end of Bassenthwaite, is generally unobtrusive, but illustrates the potential conflict between recreational interests and wildlife conservation.

Waterbirds

At any time: Little Grebe, Great Crested Grebe, Greylag Goose, Red-breasted Merganser, Goosander, Black-headed Gull.

Winter: Whooper Swan, Wigeon, Goldeneye, Pochard, storm-driven seabirds, Herring, Black-headed and Common Gull.

② BORROWDALE   Woodland

OS 1:25,000 NW Sheet/Bartholomew Lake District Map or National Sheet 34

Access: By car—South from Keswick on B5289 to Grange, or from Buttermere via Honister Pass.

Bus—Cumberland Motor Services route 79 Keswick-Seatoller.

Boat—Frequent launches ply Derwentwater—two landing stages at south end of lake.

Borrowdale probably has more semi-natural woodland than any other valley. This is generally oak-dominated with birch as a constant, if subsidiary, species and ash/elm mixtures occurring on lime-rich outcrops. Most are 'hanging woods' on steep, rocky slopes difficult to explore, but Lodore Woods and Johnny's Wood both have good access.

Birds

Spring/Summer: Buzzard, Tawny Owl, Great Spotted Woodpecker, Tree Pipit, Wood Warbler, Pied Flycatcher, Redstart, Long-tailed Tit, Coal Tit, Treecreeper.

BORROWDALE

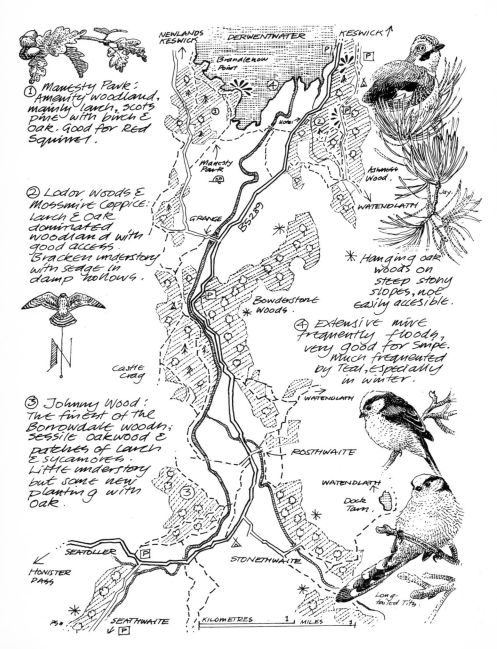

① Manesty Park: Amenity woodland, mainly larch, scots pine with birch & oak. Good for Red Squirrel.

② Lodor Woods & Mossmire Coppice: Larch & oak dominated woodland with good access. Bracken understory with sedge in damp hollows.

③ Johnny Wood: The finest of the Borrowdale woods; sessile oakwood & patches of larch & sycamores. Little understory but some new planting with oak.

* Hanging oak woods on steep stony slopes, not easily accesible.

④ Extensive mire frequently floods, very good for snipe. Much frequented by Teal, especially in winter.

NEWLANDS KESWICK
DERWENTWATER
KESWICK↑
Brandlehow Point
Manesty Park
GRANGE
B5289
Castle Crag
Bowderstone Woods.
Ashness Wood.
WATENDLATH
Jay.
WATENDLATH
ROSTHWAITE
WATENDLATH
Dock Tarn
SEATOLLER
HONISTER PASS
STONETHWAITE
Long-tailed Tits.
PS0
SEATHWAITE
KILOMETRES 1
MILES 1

N

③ BROTHERS WATER AND DOVEDALE
Lake, Upland Wood and Fell

OS 1:25,000 NE Sheet/Bartholomew Lake District Map or National Sheet 34

Access: By car—2m S. of Patterdale, 3m N. of Kirkstone Pass, on A592.

Bus—Mountain Goat minibus Ambleside-Brothers Water-Keswick. Ribble Services 559 and 649.

Brothers Water is one of the smallest low-lying lakes and permits intimate observation of its waterfowl. The north and south shores grade into mire, then rough pasture and scattered trees. Low Wood, rising steeply from the stony western shore, comprises mainly oak, with some ash, alder, holly and rowan.

Birds

Resident:	Little Grebe, Heron, Goosander, Buzzard, Snipe, Great Spotted Woodpecker, Coal and Long-tailed Tit, Nuthatch, Treecreeper, Dipper, Reed Bunting, Raven.
Spring/ Summer:	Common Sandpiper, Grey and Yellow Wagtail, Sedge Warbler, Pied Flycatcher, Whinchat, Wheatear, Redstart, Ring Ousel.
Winter and Passage	Geese, Wigeon, Shoveler, Tufted Duck, Pochard, Goldeneye, Red-breasted Merganser, Fieldfare, Redwing, Siskin, Redpoll.

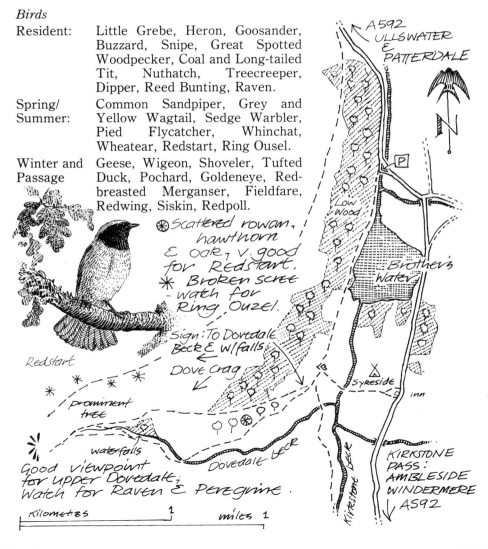

OS 1:25,000 SE Sheet/Bartholomew Lake District Map or National Sheet 34

Access: By car—A6 north from Kendal, turning left after 4m at Garnett
Bridge. Follow unclassified road up Longsleddale for 5m to Sadgill.

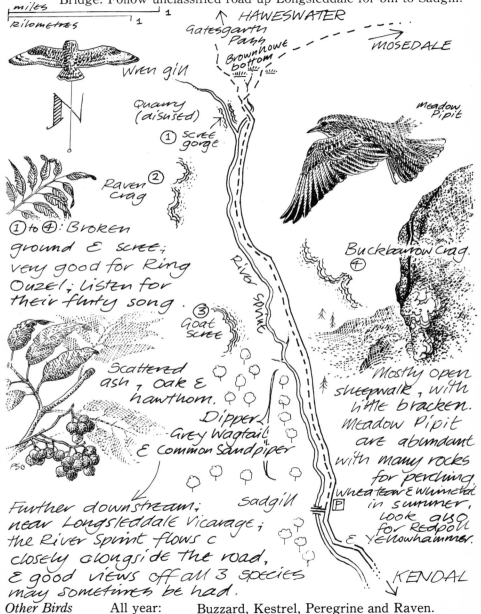

miles
kilometres

↑ HAWESWATER
Gatesgarth Pass
Brownhowe bottom
→ MOSEDALE

Wren gill

N

Quarry (disused)
① Scree gorge

Raven Crag ②

meadow Pipit

Buckbarrow Crag.
④

① to ④: Broken ground & scree; very good for Ring Ouzel; listen for their flinty song.

③ Goat Scree

River Sprint

Scattered ash, oak & hawthorn.

Dipper
Grey Wagtail
& Common Sandpiper

P30

Sadgill

P

Mostly open sheepwalk, with little bracken. Meadow Pipit are abundant with many rocks for perching. wheatear & whinchat in summer. look also for Redpoll & Yellowhammer.

Further downstream; near Longsleddale Vicarage; the River Sprint flows c closely alongside the road, & good views off all 3 species may sometimes be had.

→ KENDAL

Other Birds   All year: Buzzard, Kestrel, Peregrine and Raven.

⑤ WHITE MOSS COMMON AND RYDAL WATER

Lake and Moss

OS 1:25,000 SE Sheet/Bartholomew Lake District Map or National Sheet 34

Access: By car—2.5 miles north of Ambleside, 1.5 miles south of Grasmere, on A591 Kendal-Keswick road. Car park at White Moss.

Bus—Ribble Services 555 and 556 Keswick-Ambleside-Kendal and 518 and 520 Keswick-Rydal-Ambleside-Barrow.

The National Trust land at White Moss is one of the first places where visitors from the south can pull off the road. It annually attracts thousands of people, a situation which poses a serious threat to the relatively fragile 'moss' habitat at the lake head. Happily, recent measures to protect this site, including the laying of a fibre-glass footpath and the use of 'discreet' signposting, are proving quite successful. A complete circuit of the lake is strongly recommended, taking in the oak-dominated woodland and moss/reed fen at the western end, the south shore with its uninterrupted views of the lake, and the 'parkland' habitat to the north.

Birds

Spring/Summer: Greylag Goose, Red-breasted Merganser, Goosander (Buzzard, Peregrine and Raven over the ridge), Common Sandpiper, Grey Wagtail, Dipper, Pied Flycatcher, Spotted Flycatcher, Redstart, Nuthatch.

Winter: Whooper Swan, Pochard, Goldeneye.

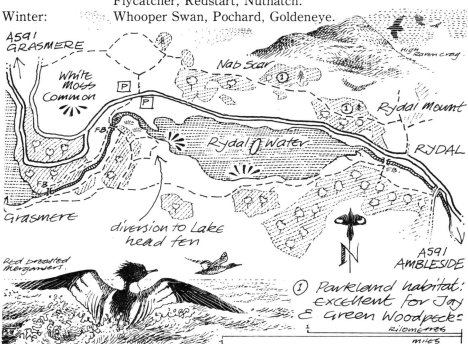

43

⑥ TILBERTHWAITE

Coppice Woodland/Fell

OS 1:25,000 SW or SE Sheet/Bart. Lake District Map or National Sheet 34

Access: By car—A593 Coniston-Ambleside road, turn left 1.5 miles north of Coniston. From Ambleside, turn right three miles past Skelwith Bridge. Parking at Gill Bridge.

Bus: Ribble Services 513 Ambleside-Coniston-Ulverston.

The scenery of Tilberthwaite derives from two traditional Lakeland industries; slate quarrying and woodland coppicing. Exploring the labyrinth of disused quarry workings around Hodge Close gives a fascinating insight into the industrial archaeology of the Lake District. The woods, now largely owned by the National Trust, comprise mainly oak and birch, with some larch stands. The woodland floor is generally damp and mossy, with very little secondary vegetation, and this discourages shyer birds such as the warblers, which favour dense thicket cover. Woodcock prefer it, however, and in winter are reasonably common here.

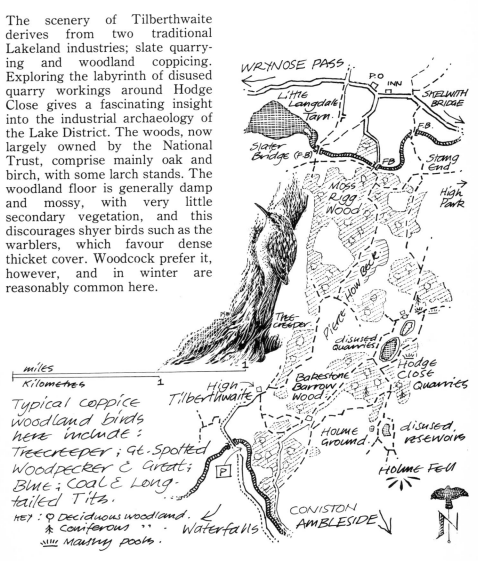

WRYNOSE PASS
P.O
INN
SKELWITH BRIDGE
Little Langdale Tarn
F.B.
Slater Bridge (F.B)
F.B
Stang End
High Park
Moss Rigg Wood
Pierce How Beck
Tree-creeper
disused Quarries
Hodge Close Quarries
miles
Kilometres
1
High Tilberthwaite
Bakestone Barrow Wood
Holme Ground
disused reservoirs
P
Holme Fell
CONISTON AMBLESIDE
N

Typical coppice woodland birds here include: Treecreeper; Gt. Spotted Woodpecker & Great; Blue; Coal & Long-tailed Tits.

KEY: ♀ Deciduous woodland. ↙ Waterfalls
↟ Coniferous " .
⸬⸬ Marshy pools.

44

If ascending Holme Fell, a fine viewpoint for Coniston Water, note the transition from larch woodland, through the heather and juniper habitat surrounding the reservoirs, and into the heather/bracken mix of the fell summit.

Birds

Resident: Buzzard, Kestrel, Tawny Owl, Great Spotted Woodpecker, Jay, Dipper, tits, Treecreeper.

Spring/Summer: Meadow Pipit, Tree Pipit, Grey Wagtail, Willow Warbler, Pied Flycatcher, Redstart.

⑦ BROCKHOLE   National Park Visitor Centre

OS 1:25,000 SE Sheet/Bartholomew Lake District Map or National Sheet 34

Access: By car—A591 Windermere-Ambleside road. Ample parking.

Bus—Ribble Services 517-521, 555, 556 and 558 Windermere-Brockhole-Ambleside.

Admission Charge

Brockhole is the Lake District National Park Visitor Centre. It is open daily from late March until early November and offers a large programme of audio-visual presentations, talks, short courses and permanent exhibitions featuring

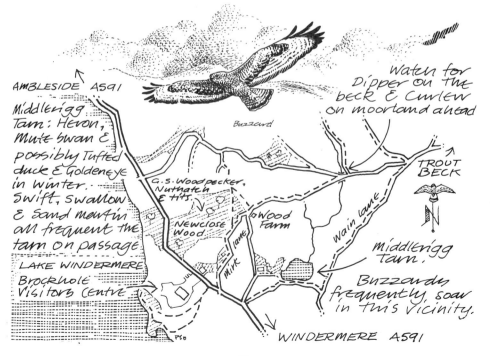

AMBLESIDE A591

Middlerigg Tarn: Heron, Mute Swan & possibly Tufted duck & Goldeneye in winter. Swift, swallow & Sand martin all frequent the tarn on passage.

LAKE WINDERMERE

Brockhole Visitors Centre

Buzzard

G.S. Woodpecker, Nuthatch & tits.

Newclose Wood

Wood Farm

Mirk lane

Wain lane

Watch for Dipper on the beck & Curlew on moorland ahead

TROUT BECK

Middlerigg Tarn.

Buzzards frequently soar in this vicinity.

WINDERMERE A591

45

the Lake District environment. The Centre has many displays and lectures specific to Lakeland birdlife, but more importantly, Brockhole seeks to describe the diverse habitats within the Park and explain some of the processes that create, maintain, or destroy particular landscapes. Brockhole is frequently regarded as an 'indoor alternative' in wet weather by visiting hill walkers, which is a pity, since both the extensive grounds, with their lake frontage, and the surrounding countryside, as seen for example on the Wain Lane walk, are worthy of thorough exploration.

Plenty of information concerning the grounds is available at the Centre and requires no repetition here, although mention should be made of two birds of particular interest; Pied Flycatchers, which now breed in nest boxes provided by the Cumbria Trust for Nature Conservation, and Nuthatch, whose numbers have noticeably increased during the last decade.

⑧ CLAIFE HEIGHTS   Coniferous Plantation, Lake and Tarn

OS 1:25,000 SE Sheet/Bartholomew Lake District Map or National Sheet 34

Access: By car—B5286 Hawkshead-Ambleside road, turn off to High Wray, then by narrow road to Red Nab (parking). Alternatively, take the B5285 Hawkshead-Windermere ferry road, parking at Far Sawrey.

Bus—Ribble Services 512 Ambleside-Hawkshead, 515 Ambleside-Hawkshead-Ferry Landing.

Green Woodpeckers

46

CLAIFE HEIGHTS

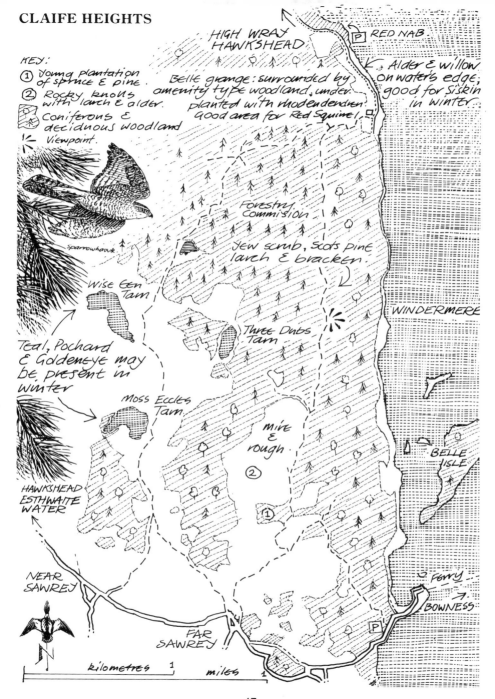

KEY:
① Young plantation of spruce & pine.
② Rocky knolls with larch & alder.
Coniferous & deciduous woodland
Viewpoint.

HIGH WRAY
HAWKSHEAD

RED NAB

Belle Grange: surrounded by amenity type woodland. under planted with rhododendron. Good area for Red Squirrel.

Alder & willow on water's edge, good for Siskin in winter.

sparrowhawk

Forestry Commission

Yew scrub, Scots pine larch & bracken.

Wise Een Tarn

Teal, Pochard & Goldeneye may be present in winter

Three Dubs Tarn

WINDERMERE

Moss Eccles Tarn

mire & rough

②

BELLE ISLE

HAWKSHEAD ESTHWAITE WATER

①

NEAR SAWREY

Ferry

BOWNESS

FAR SAWREY

N

kilometres   1
        miles   1

47

A varied area, with several types of woodland habitat, including quite extensive coniferous plantation.

Birds

Resident: Sparrowhawk, Buzzard, Woodpigeon (massive flocks can sometimes be seen in winter), Green Woodpecker, Jay, Goldcrest, Long-tailed Tit, Coal Tit, Treecreeper, Redpoll.

Summer only: Willow Warbler, Spotted Flycatcher, Wheatear.

WHITBARROW SCAR

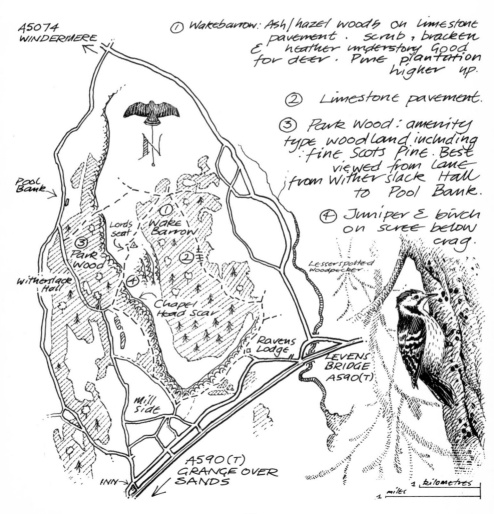

A5074 WINDERMERE

① Wakebarrow: Ash/hazel woods on limestone pavement. scrub, bracken & heather understory Good for deer. Pine plantation higher up.

② Limestone pavement.

③ Park Wood: amenity type woodland including fine Scots Pine. Best viewed from lane from Witherslack Hall to Pool Bank.

④ Juniper & birch on scree below crag.

Pool Bank

Lords seat

① Wake Barrow

③ Park Wood

Witherslack Hall

④

②

Lesser spotted Woodpecker

Chapel Head Scar

Ravens Lodge

LEVENS BRIDGE A590(T)

Mill Side

A590(T) GRANGE OVER SANDS

INN

1 kilometres
1 miles

48

⑨ WHITBARROW SCAR   Crag and Ash/Hazel Woodland

OS 1:50,000 Sheet 97/Bartholomew Lake District Map or National Sheet 34

Access: By car—A590, turn off to Mill Side. Parking on right.
        Bus—Ribble Services 530-539 Kendal-Witherslack-Ulverston.

An abrupt limestone ridge rising over 200 metres above the peat mosses of the Kent. The summit plateau, a Cumbria Trust for Nature Conservation reserve, commands superb views of the Winster valley and Kent estuary.

Birds

All year: Sparrowhawk, Buzzard, Peregrine, Woodcock, Jay, Marsh and Willow Tit.

Summer only: Garden Warbler, Blackcap, Whitethroat, Ring Ousel.

⑩ MORECAMBE BAY   Estuary, Saltmarsh and Inter-tidal mud

OS 1:50,000 Sheets 96 and 97/Bartholomew National Sheets 34 and 31

Access: By car—see map.
        Bus—Ribble Services 530-539 Kendal-Grange-Ulverston-Barrow and 544-549 Lindale-Grange-Cartmel.

1 *South Walney*. See Page 52.

2 *Cavendish Dock*. Warm, sheltered water attracts duck and seabirds in winter. Divers, Black-necked and Slavonian Grebe regularly reported. Large numbers of Little and Great Crested Grebe, Cormorant, Mute Swan, Pochard, Tufted Duck and Coot.

3 *Foulney Island*. Terns in spring, including occasional Roseate. Roosting waders on all high tides, ducks and seabirds offshore.

4 *Wadhead Scar*. High tide wader roost on shingle bank, best on moderate tides. Offshore duck, including occasional Scaup.

5 *Canal Foot*. Lookout point for middle reaches of Leven estuary. Few waders, but good for duck, including occasional Long-tailed, Duck. Also *Plumpton Hall*—footpath under the railway gives access to the upper estuary, a good area for waders. Particularly attractive to freshwater waders, such as Greenshank, Common and Green Sandpiper, on autumn passage.

6 *Park Head*. Viewpoint for east shore of estuary above viaduct. Shelduck, Mallard, Teal and Goldeneye plus vast roost of Black-headed and Common Gulls in winter. Small wader roost on average high tides. Roudsea Wood and Deer Dike Moss are both exceptional habitats to the north. The latter can be glimpsed from the B5278. Access to Roudsea is by NCC permit.

7 *Sandgate Marsh*. Very large saltmarsh. Wader roost on moderate tides. Good area for Pintail and Wigeon.

MORECAMBE BAY

Typical Birds of Morecambe Bay

Winter waterfowl:	Cormorant, Heron, Pink-footed Goose, Greylag Goose, Shelduck, Wigeon, Teal, Mallard, Pintail, Eider, Common Scoter, Goldeneye, Red-breasted Merganser.
Winter waders:	Oystercatcher, Ringed Plover, Golden and Grey Plover, Lapwing, Knot, Sanderling, Dunlin, Bar-tailed Godwit, Curlew, Redshank, Greenshank, Turnstone.

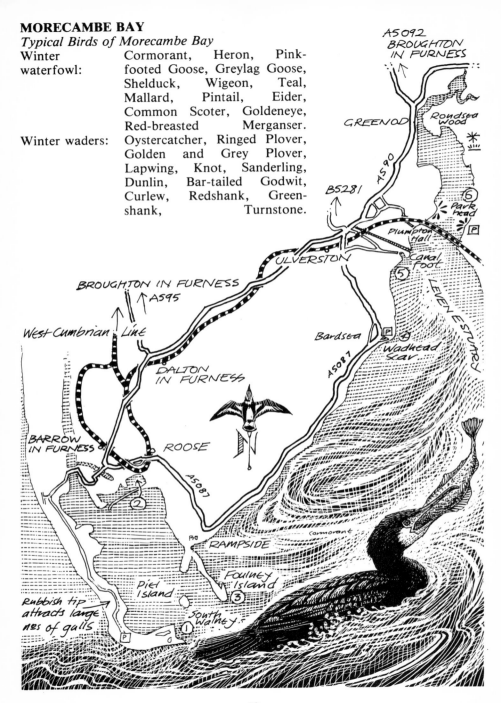

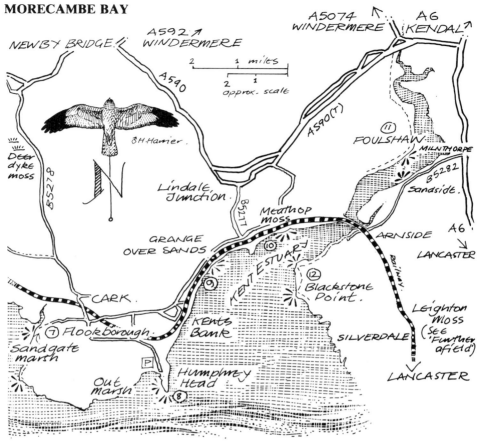

8 *Humphrey Head.* Large wader roost on very high tides. Some duck; Shelduck abundant. Outmarsh is a favoured haunt of passage Whimbrel.

9 *Kents Bank to Grange.* Promenade and footpath. Extensive area of inter-tidal sand and mud for wader feeding. Usually good numbers of Shelduck, Pintail and Goldeneye.

10 *Meathop Moss.* Former raised peat bog, now largely drained. Occasional passage harriers.

11 *Foulshaw.* Footpath along sea wall gives good views of upper Kent estuary. Feeding waders at low tide; good roosts only on very high tides. Large Common and Black-headed Gull roost. Brackish saltmarsh pools sometimes hold rarer waders in spring/autumn.

12 *Blackstone Point.* Footpath westwards from Arnside to New Barns and Blackstone Point gives views of lower Kent. Continue to Far Arnside for views over Silverdale Marsh; Shelduck, Wigeon, Pintail, occasional geese, wader roost on moderate tides.

OS 1:50,000 Sheet 96/Bartholomew National Sheet 31

Access: By car—From Barrow, follow Walney Island signs. Once on the Island turn left for ½ mile, then left again and head south for five miles. Parking at reserve entrance.

The reserve is closed on Mondays.

Walney Bird Observatory is situated at the southernmost tip of Walney Island. It forms the southwest corner of the Lake District and is the most westerly extreme of Morecambe Bay, factors which, combined, result in South Walney having the largest throughput of recorded migratory birds in Cumbria, with over 210 species having been observed. The reserve is managed by the Cumbria Trust for Nature Conservation who levy a modest entrance charge.

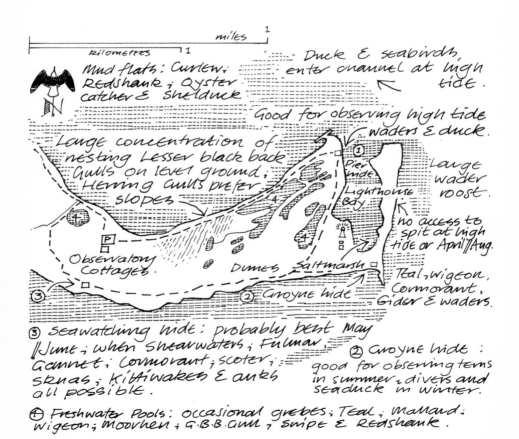

miles 1

kilometres 1

Mud flats: Curlew; Redshank; Oyster catcher & Shelduck

Duck & seabirds, enter channel at high tide.

Good for observing high tide waders & duck.

Large concentration of nesting Lesser black back Gulls on level ground; Herring Gulls prefer slopes

Pier hide

① Large wader roost.

Lighthouse Bay

no access to spit at high tide or April/Aug.

Observatory Cottages.

Dunes Saltmarsh

② Groyne hide

Teal, wigeon, Cormorant, Eider & waders.

③ Seawatching hide: probably best May/June; when Shearwaters; Fulmar; Gannet; Cormorant; scoter; skuas; kittiwakes & auks all possible.

② Groyne hide: good for observing terns in summer, divers and seaduck in winter.

④ Freshwater Pools: occasional grebes; Teal; Mallard; wigeon; Moorhen; G.B.B. Gull; Snipe & Redshank.

Birds

Breeding:
Over 30,000 pairs Lesser Black-backed and Herring Gull. Shelduck, Eider, Oystercatcher, Ringed Plover and occasional terns.

Spring and autumn migrants:
Wealth of waders and passerines, including annual rarities. Regular Osprey, Little Stint, Curlew Sandpiper, Ruff, Bar-tailed Godwit, Whimbrel, Spotted Redshank, Greenshank, Green, Wood and Common Sandpiper, Turnstone, Sandwich, Common, Arctic and Little Terns, Short-eared Owl, wagtails, chats, Wheatear, warblers, Linnet.

Recent rarities include Buff-breasted Sandpiper, a dowitcher species, Richard's and Tawny Pipits, Icterine, Melodious, Barred and Yellow-browed Warblers, Paddyfield Warbler, Nutcracker and White-throated Sparrow.

Winter:
As for Morecambe Bay, plus regular divers, grebes, Scaup, Purple Sandpiper, Glaucous Gull, Black Redstart, Twite, Snow Bunting.

Eider Duck

⑫ DUDDON ESTUARY AND ANGERTON MOSS

Estuary and Moss

OS 1:50,000 Sheet 96/Bartholomew National Sheet 34

Access: By car—Two miles south of Broughton-in-Furness, on A595 Barrow-Workington road. Park at Foxfield.

By rail—West Cumbria Line to Foxfield Station.

Bus—Ribble Services 502 and 511 Ulverston-Foxfield-Millom and 513 Ambleside-Foxfield-Ulverston.

A fine combination of estuarine and heathland habitat. Try to time your arrival at Whelpshead Crag for about 1½ hours before a very high tide; the waders will then be pushed towards you by the advancing tideline. Watch the state of the tide at all times, especially if venturing out onto Duddon Sands. Tide tables are available from local booksellers (*see* Useful Addresses).

DUDDON ESTUARY AND ANGERTON MOSS

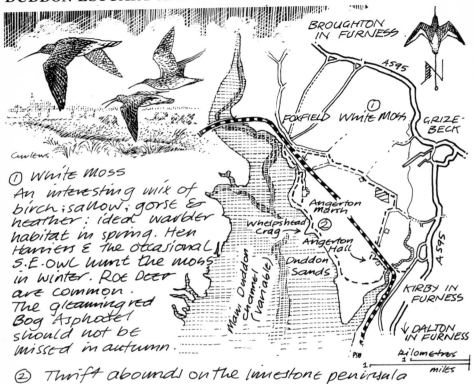

BROUGHTON
IN FURNESS

A595

FOXFIELD ① White Moss GRIZE-BECK

Angerton Marsh

Whelpshead Crag → ②
Angerton Hall →

Duddon Sands

Main Duddon Channel (variable)

Curlews

① White Moss
An interesting mix of birch, sallow, gorse & heather: ideal warbler habitat in spring. Hen Harriers & the occasional S.E.Owl hunt the moss in winter. Roe Deer are common. The gleaming red Bog Asphodel should not be missed in autumn.

② Thrift abounds on the limestone peninsula

KIRBY IN FURNESS

↓ DALTON IN FURNESS

kilometres

miles

Birds

Resident:	Shelduck, Greylag Goose, Red-breasted Merganser, Stonechat, Reed Bunting.
Summer:	Lesser Black-backed Gull, terns, Nightjar, Grasshopper Warbler, Sedge Warbler, Whitethroat, Wheatear.
Passage:	Hen Harrier, Golden and Grey Plover, Knot, Ruff, godwits, Spotted Redshank, Greenshank, Green Sandpiper, Common Sandpiper.
Winter:	Wigeon, Pintail (usually good numbers), Hen Harrier, Merlin, Peregrine, Jack Snipe, Short-eared Owl, occasional Brambling.

Amongst less usual birds seen here in recent years are Little Egret, Long-tailed Duck and Red-necked Phalarope.

OS 1:50,000 Sheet 96/Bartholomew National Sheet 34

Access: By car—A5093 to Millom. Turn right off Devonshire Road onto
Mainsgate Road, park at end; or approach from Haverigg, one mile
SW of Millom.

By rail—West Cumbria Line to Millom.

Bus—Ribble Services 502 and 511 Ulverston-Millom.
Cumberland Motor Services route 12 Whitehaven-Seascale-Millom.

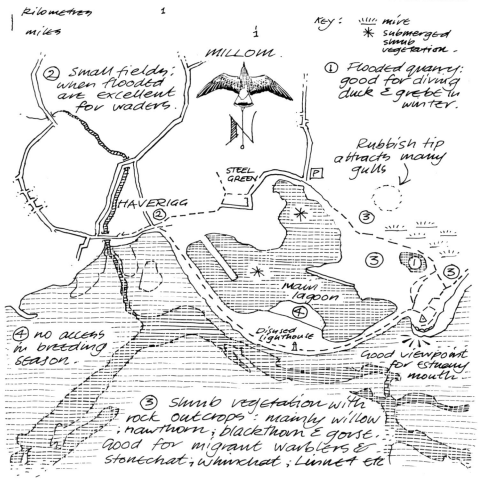

Kilometres 1
miles 1

Key: 〰 mire
✳ submerged shrub vegetation.

MILLOM.

② Small fields; when flooded are excellent for waders.

① Flooded quarry: good for diving duck & grebe in winter.

Rubbish tip attracts many gulls

STEEL GREEN

HAVERIGG ②

③

③

③

Main lagoon

④

Disused lighthouse

④ no access in breeding season.

Good viewpoint for estuary mouth.

③ shrub vegetation with rock outcrops: mainly willow; hawthorn; blackthorn & gorse. Good for migrant warblers & stonechat; whinchat; Linnet etc

Hodbarrow is an outstanding example of first-rate habitat created from former
industrial land. Situated adjacent to the Duddon estuary and the open sea, the
main lagoon and smaller pools are valuable havens for storm-driven duck, as

well as important freshwater habitats in their own right. The derelict landscape is overgrown with shrubs and pioneer vegetation which attracts many migrants using the western coast route, recently including White Wagtail, Lesser Whitethroat and Black Redstart. Seawatching can be good; Scaup are present all year, skuas often enter the estuary mouth and shearwater passages are regular, if distant.

Hodbarrow is under increasing threat of re-development and the first phase of a holiday complex is already near completion. It will be sad if this fine habitat is lost completely to recreational use and it is to be hoped that some conservation strategy will be incorporated into the development scheme.

Birds

Spring/Summer: Up to 300 post-breeding Red-breasted Merganser (July), up to 100 Common Scoter, Coot, Sandwich, Common, Arctic and Little Tern, migrant passerines.

Regular waders: Golden Plover, Sanderling, Dunlin, Greenshank, Ruff, Whimbrel, godwits.

Winter: Red-throated and Black-throated Diver, Little Grebe, Great Crested Grebe, Black-necked Grebe, Whooper Swan, Wigeon, Teal, Pintail (up to 250 on estuary), Pochard, Tufted Duck, Scaup, Long-tailed Duck, Goldeneye, Sparrowhawk, Peregrine, Merlin.

Arctic Terns

⑭ RAVENGLASS (i.e. the Esk, Mite and Irt estuaries)

The confluence of these three rivers at Ravenglass gives rise to a complex topography, with a varied mix of sand dune, saltmarsh and inter-tidal mud, backed by farmland habitat. Two peninsulas guard the estuaries: Eskmeals Dunes to the south, a Cumbria Trust for Nature Conservation reserve, and Drigg Dunes to the north, managed as a nature reserve by Cumbria County Council.

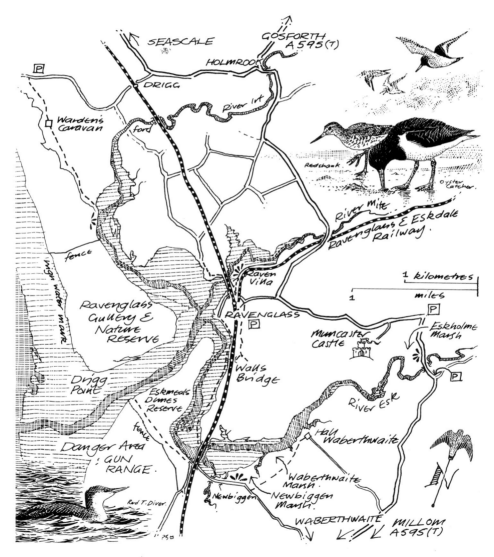

OS 1:25,000 SW Sheet/Bartholomew National Sheet 34

Access: By car—A595 to Waberthwaite, then minor road via Newbiggin to viaduct (road flooded at high tide), or A595 to Bootle, then minor road via Bootle Station to viaduct. Parking nearby.

No permits required.

West of the railway viaduct the southern shore of the Esk becomes Eskmeals Dunes, a sandy spit extending northwards to oppose Drigg peninsula. The channel between the two is of particular interest, although the Cumbria Trust for Nature Conservation reserve, comprising the whole of the northern dune system, should not be missed. The reserve is entered by following the shore westwards from the viaduct; then cross the dunes on a track which keeps a course parallel to the Gun Range boundary fence. Periodic blasts from the range elicit surprisingly little reaction from the resident birds. The scrub vegetation here is predominantly sea buckthorn; good for warblers in spring (Lesser Whitethroat is regular) and for Fieldfare in winter.

The track emerges onto the shore of the main channel which drains the Esk, Mite and Irt rivers. This can be good at any time, but a visit in early summer is best for seeing fishing terns, whilst during the foulest of westerly winter gales (and shortly afterwards) sea duck and divers sometimes shelter in the channel. A return round the end of the spit is recommended; the stony shoreline encountered initially holds Turnstone in winter. The sandy channels of the Esk should be scanned for duck and waders, although they are not generally as productive as the Irt.

Birds

Summer: Red-breasted Merganser, Sandwich, Common, Arctic and Little Tern, Cuckoo, Skylark, Stonechat, Wheatear.

Grey Heron

Passage at sea: Shearwaters, Gannet, skuas (often enter channel to harass gulls and terns).

Winter: Red-throated and Great Northern Diver, Eider, Common Scoter, Goldeneye, Oystercatcher (massive roost on Drigg side of channel), Turnstone, Dunlin, Fieldfare.

Other good areas:

1 *Mite Estuary*. Secluded estuary north of Ravenglass, behind viaduct. Best scanned with a telescope from the shore near Raven Villa, accessible from an opening opposite entrance to the Ravenglass and Eskdale Railway station. Quite good for waders.

2 *Ravenglass Shore*. Stony shoreline south of 'slipway' at the end of Main Street. Good for Turnstone and occasional Purple Sandpiper in winter. Good views, too, of the Esk estuary. Pass under railway at Walls Bridge and return through Walls Plantation.

3 *Eskholme Marsh*. Unimproved saltmarsh pasture mostly to seaward side of A595. Best viewed from roadside, although parking is awkward (see map). The main attraction is the flock of 100 or so resident Greylag Geese which sometimes feed and roost here. Lately, odd Barnacle, Canada and Pink-footed Geese have accompanied the flock, these being feral or injured individuals. (At the time of writing the flock includes an Egyptian Goose!) Curlews are numerous, as are Grey Heron from the nearby Muncaster heronry. Kingfisher are regular near the bridge.

4 *Newbiggin Marsh*. On south shore of Esk between Newbiggin and viaduct (road submerged at high tide). Again, best viewed from the road, perhaps using your car as a hide. Up to 200 Wigeon in winter, large numbers of Redshank, occasional Greenshank and godwits. Marshy fields behind road can be good for passage sandpipers and hold Snipe throughout the year.

Wigeon

OS 1:25,000 SW Sheet/Bartholomew National Sheet 34

Access: By car—B5344 Holmrook-Seascale road, turning left at Drigg. Parking at Drigg foreshore (one mile).

By rail—West Cumbria Line to Drigg Station.

Bus—Cumberland Motor Services route 12 Whitehaven-Seascale-Millom. Alight at Drigg.

Entrance by permit only, obtainable from: County Land Surveyor, Aroyo Block, The Castle, Carlisle.

Approaching along the Drigg Shore road, watch for Sparrowhawks and Little Owls perching on fence posts bordering the conifers to the right. The reserve lies south of Drigg road end (a good seawatching point during westerly gales). In the breeding season, the warden may instruct you to avoid those parts of the reserve where birds are nesting. Otherwise it is possible to walk to the far end of the peninsula along a waymarked route.

The Irt estuary is best scanned from the central part of the spit, where the track closely follows the water's edge, but lack of cover prevents close observation of any duck and a telescope will be required for careful identification of small waders. The saltmarsh opposite continues as far as Drigg Ford and is probably the most important high tide wader roost on the Esk-Mite-Irt complex. Passage birds are generally best in autumn, although recent spring records have included Spoonbill and Red-necked Phalarope.

Beyond the fence across the dunes lie the main gull breeding grounds; Drigg at one time boasted the largest Black-headed Gull colony in Britain. Herring and Lesser Black-backed Gull also breed. Nesting tern have had varying fortunes, suffering considerably from predators such as crows, gulls, fox, stoat and mink. Disturbance from passing boats has probably contributed to their decline.

In summer, time your arrival at the far end of the dunes to coincide with a high tide, when migratory terns may move up the main channel of the Esk seeking fish.

Birds

All year:	Cormorant, Heron, Greylag Goose, Shelduck, Red-breasted Merganser, Teal, Sparrowhawk, Kestrel, Oystercatcher, Redshank, Dunlin, Ringed Plover, Snipe, Curlew, gulls.
Summer:	Lesser Black-backed Gull, Common, Arctic, Sandwich and Little Terns.
Winter:	Whooper Swan, Pink-footed Goose, Wigeon, Goldeneye, Peregrine, Merlin, Turnstone.
Passage waders:	Common and Green Sandpipers, Spotted Redshank, Greenshank, Little Stint, Sanderling, Golden and Grey Plover, godwits, Whimbrel.

⑮ DALEGARTH WOODS Amenity woodland

OS 1:25,000 SW Sheet/Bartholomew Lake District Map or National Sheet 34

Access: By car—Two miles up valley from Eskdale Green, turn right 1.5 miles after King George IV Inn. From Ambleside via Wrynose and Hardknott Pass, turn left ½m past Eskdale Stn. Car park at Trough House Bridge.

By rail—Narrow gauge railway from Ravenglass to Eskdale Station.

Bus—Mountain Goat Windermere-Ambleside-Wasdale route stops at Eskdale Station.

Birdwatching immediately around the car park can be good; I have seen Tawny Owl, roe deer and fox in the early morning. Backtrack to Trough House Bridge for Dipper and Common Sandpiper.

Around Stanley Ghyll are fine exotic trees planted during the 17th and 18th centuries. The tree canopy here is so high that locating birds can be quite difficult. The ghyll itself should be visited primarily for scenic interest although Grey Wagtails may be present below the falls. Note that no exit is feasible beyond the gorge. Instead, take the path rising steeply from just below the top bridge to join the path leading to the top of the falls. From here, a stile leads on to the open fell, and to the west a track down to Dalegarth will be apparent. The parkland-type habitat opposite St Catherine's Church, and the deciduous woods towards Forge Bridge, are also particularly worthy of attention.

Grey Wagtail

61

Birds

Spring/Summer:
  Garden and Wood Warbler, Pied Flycatcher, Redstart.

Resident:
  Buzzard, Kestrel, Great Spotted Woodpecker, Goldcrest, Coal and Long-tailed Tit, Nuthatch, Treecreeper.

Winter:
  Siskin, Redpoll.

DEVOKE WATER   Upland Tarn and Moorland

OS 1:25,000 SW Sheet/Bartholomew Lake District Map or National Sheet 34

Access: By car—Park at summit of Ulpha-Eskdale Green road. Track to Devoke signposted 'Bridleway to Waberthwaite'. Alternatively, an interesting walk from Dalegarth Woods can be devised.

Devoke Water, a large natural hill tarn stocked with Brown Trout, lies at an altitude of 250m on the moorland plateau of Birker Fell. Approaching along the track to Waberthwaite, strong afternoon sunlight may reduce views of waterfowl to mere silhouettes, in which case, although the going will be boggy underfoot, a circuit of the lake is recommended. To the north, heather moor blanketing Rough and Water Crags provides good cover for Red Grouse and is occasionally hunted over by Merlins.

Birds

Spring/Summer: Osprey on passage, Common Sandpiper, Meadow Pipit, Wheatear.

Winter: Occasional divers, Cormorant, Whooper Swan, Pochard, Goldeneye, Pink-footed Goose, occasional Hen Harrier.

At any time: Grey Heron, Greylag Goose, Canada Goose, Tufted Duck, Red-breasted Merganser, Goosander, Snipe, Curlew, Red Grouse, Merlin, Kestrel.

Osprey

OS 1:50,000 Sheet 89/Bartholomew National Sheet 34

Access: By car—Beach road from St Bees village. Car park. Cars are *not* allowed along the Sandwith-North Head road.

By rail—West Cumbria Line to St Bees.

Bus—Cumberland Motor Services route 03 Whitehaven-Sandwith and route 20 Whitehaven-St Bees-Egremont.

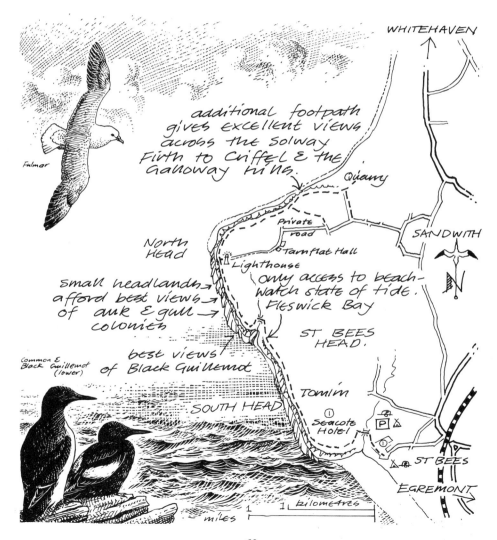

The red sandstone cliffs of St Bees hold over 5000 breeding seabirds, the largest colony on the west coast of England. Substantial stretches of the 100m high cliffs are owned by the RSPB which employs a warden throughout the breeding season. This is the only place in mainland England where Black Guillemot breed, although some 50 pairs breed on the Isle of Man. The best area to see one of the dozen or so Puffins is from the first viewpoint south of the lighthouse. The reserve is at its best in spring when, not only the nesting seabirds, but also many migrant species can be seen.

a) Jackdaw b) imm. & adult c) Kittiwake
d) Puffin e) Cormorant f) Razorbill

Birds

Breeding: Fulmar, Kittiwake, Guillemot, Razorbill, Black Guillemot, Puffin, Feral Pigeon, Little Owl, Rock Pipit.

Seawatching can be rewarding; good tern and Gannet passages occur in May, although the shearwaters and occasional skuas tend to be rather distant.

Recent spring rarities include Chough, Black Redstart, Twite, White Wagtail, Whimbrel and Wood Sandpiper.

LONGLANDS   Inland pool

OS 1:50,000 Sheet 89/Bartholomew National Sheet 34

Access: By car—A5086 Egremont-Cockermouth road; turn off just south of Cleator (signposted 'Longlands Lake'). Car parking space provided.
Bus—Cumberland Motor Services routes 12 and 20 Whitehaven-Egremont and route 22 Whitehaven-Cleator-Egremont.

This little known small lake one mile north of Egremont can be conveniently included in a visit to St Bees Head. Crossing the River Ehen, look for Dippers and Grey Wagtails, both of which breed here. The pool holds several duck species, including Pochard and Goldeneye in winter. Great Crested and Little Grebes are usually present. Sand Martin, Common and Arctic Terns are annual migrant visitors, and Green Sandpiper and Black Tern were recorded recently. Both Peregrine and Merlin are possible in winter, in addition to the resident Kestrel.

SIDDICK PONDS   Inland pool and reed fen
OS 1:50,000 Sheet 89/Bartholomew National Sheet 34

Access: By car—A596 Workington-Carlisle road, parking 1½m N. of Workington on Council land on the left just before Thames Board mill.

By bus: Cumberland Motor Services route 30 Whitehaven-Carlisle, alight at Siddick.

Formerly part of the River Derwent estuary, Siddick Ponds now comprise 22 acres of open water with an extensive phragmites reed bed at the south-eastern end. Access to the site is restricted; the best views are from the railway line, but this is still in occasional use. Permission to use the hide near the road should be sought from the honorary warden, Mr J C Callion, The Cherries, Scawfield, High Harrington, Tel. Harrington 830651.

Birds
Breeding: Tufted Duck, Grasshopper, Sedge and Reed Warblers, Blackcap.
Migrants: Ruff, godwits, sandpipers, Black Tern.
Winter: Whooper Swan, Goldeneye and other winter duck, Short-eared Owl.
A large Starling roost in autumn attracts raptors such as Peregrine and Merlin.

Further afield:

LEIGHTON MOSS

Those approaching the Lake District from the south should not miss the RSPB reserve at Leighton Moss. Leave the M6 at Junction 35 and follow the A6 for 3 miles towards Kendal. Turn left for Yealand Redmayne, followed by a right then left turn which brings you to the reserve entrance, car park and information centre, ¼ mile short of Silverdale Station.

Leighton Moss comprises three large but shallow meres, surrounded by extensive reed beds. At the western end these merge into saltmarsh, whilst towards the east a succession from open water through reed fen to mature woodland occurs. The drier fen is characterised by sedges and rushes, with groups of willow and occasional alder and hawthorn. Some willow scrub areas are being superseded by oak, ash and birch. Over 200 species of bird have been recorded here, and 74 of them have bred. Most notable of these are the ten or so pairs of breeding Bittern. Skulking birds, they are probably easiest to see in May/June, when their demanding young force the adults to become more active. Bearded Tits also breed here—these too can be difficult to locate in the reeds, but seem more confiding early in the day.

Of special interest

Breeding:	Bittern, Garganey (becoming scarcer), Shoveler, Pochard, Water Rail, Spotted Crake (two occasions only), Marsh Tit, Bearded Tit, Grasshopper Warbler, Reed Warbler, Sedge Warbler, Lesser Whitethroat, Reed Bunting.
Spring passage:	Marsh Harrier and Osprey (both regular).Occasional rarities such as Purple Heron and Spoonbill.
Autumn passage:	Waders—Spotted Redshank, Greenshank, Ruff, Wood and Green Sandpiper.
Winter:	Wildfowl—Teal, Wigeon, Pintail, Shoveler, Goldeneye, occasional Whooper and Bewick's Swan.

There is a public footpath across the reserve and a hide open to the public at all times. Access to the remaining area is by permit only (at present free to RSPB members), obtainable from the information centre or from RSPB headquarters (*see* Addresses).

Present opening times: April-September: Sat, Sun, Wed and Thur
                               October-January: Wed and Sun
                               February and March: Wed, Sat and Sun.

SOUTH SOLWAY

Two areas are of interest: Moricambe Bay, fed by the rivers Wampool and Waver, and the inner firth of the Solway, i.e. between Port Carlisle and Rockcliffe. Grune Point, the best known birdwatching area for Moricambe Bay, is approached from Silloth along an unclassified road to Skinburness. From here it is only a short walk to the point. Alternatively, drive to Kirkbride on the B5307 and turn off towards Cardurnock. This road gives good views of the River Wampool, especially near Anthorn, but westerly sunlight may prove a nuisance after mid-day. Continuing on this road through Bowness and Port Carlisle, one reaches the inner firth area. The main channel of the Eden usually runs close to the South Solway shore here, however, and getting close views of waders therefore presents quite a problem. At Burgh-by-Sands, turn left and locate a footpath leading to a monument to Edward I. Beyond the monument is the eastern edge of Burgh Marsh and from here a view is obtained of Rockcliffe Marsh, a very important area for wintering waders and geese.

Both the Moricambe and inner firth areas are heavily shot over, but are regular haunts of wintering wildfowl and waders.

Birds

Winter:	Occasional divers, Pink-footed Goose, Barnacle Goose, Shelduck, Wigeon, Teal, Pintail, Shoveler, Scaup, Eider, Long-tailed Duck, Red-breasted Merganser, Hen Harrier, Peregrine, Merlin, Oystercatcher, Ringed Plover, Golden* and Grey Plover, Lapwing*, Knot, Sanderling, Black-tailed and Bar-tailed Godwit, Whimbrel, Greenshank, Turnstone.

* Among the largest estuarine flocks in Britain.

CONSERVATION AND THE FUTURE

Visiting the Lake District is for many people a means of escaping from the daily stresses of their working environment. It can be very hard to convince such people that Lakeland life, too, has its pressures and that the environment faces many problems, not the least being that of coping with the numbers of visitors now attracted to this 'recreational paradise'.

In social terms, the Lake District is without doubt one of the more economically handicapped and least prosperous parts of England, having relatively low incomes, high unemployment and a great dependence upon seasonal work and primary industries, such as agriculture and forestry. Its population is currently aging, due in part to an incoming flow of retired people, but also to the migration of younger people seeking employment and higher living standards.

Environmentally, the conditions are some of the harshest in England and the vegetation and associated wildlife consequently less diverse than in more climatically favourable areas. The flora and fauna tend to be very susceptible to damage as a result of insensitive land use and the acidic soils, harsh climate and short growing season limit the propensity of many Lake District ecosystems for self-renewal and repair.

Wastwater

Kestrel & Ravens

Several 'direct' threats facing Lakeland birdlife have been discussed previously and disturbance to breeding birds by activities such as walking, climbing, sailing, canoeing and power boating are all obvious problems often requiring localised solutions. A traditional problem in nearly all rural areas is the attitude of farmers, landowners and gamekeepers to natural predators, and although the instances of deliberate trapping and shooting of protected species have declined in England, the illegal use of unselective poisons to control crows and foxes is still prevalent. More topical concerns are the spread of mink to many Lakeland valleys, the disturbance caused by low-flying aircraft and the acidification of many of our rivers due to airborne pollution. The latter may have been responsible for the drastic decline in salmon and trout catches in recent years and this may affect the status of the Dipper too if the diversity of aquatic insect life becomes reduced.

Industrial and housing development within the National Park is generally on such a small scale that it causes little significant habitat loss, but major changes have been wrought by civil engineering works; for example, the creation of reservoirs such as Thirlmere and Haweswater, and the improvement of many Lakeland roads. Future threats of this nature include schemes such as the Morecambe Bay barrage and the underground storage of radioactive waste. The natural landscape of the Lake District is perhaps less threatened, however, by these local, if cataclysmic, changes than by the widespread yet insidious changes in modern agriculture and forestry.

Cumbrian hill farmers have received subsidies in the form of annual payments per head of livestock and favourable grants on large-scale capital investment for the past 40 years, factors which have encouraged the over-stocking of land with sheep and the demise of the small, less economic farms as amalgamation has created fewer but larger units. This system of support continued virtually unaltered when Britain entered the EEC, except that payments were made in accordance with EEC directives on less favoured areas and farm modernisation. The social and environmental aims of these directives, however, differ fundamentally from the basically agricultural aims of the UK policies, which are designed to increase output and profit per man and improve the living standards of the remaining farmers and farm workers without unduly increasing prices to consumers.

Similar economic considerations have been used to encourage the establishment of quick-return coniferous plantations in the uplands, despite an appalling lack of evidence as to the long-term ecological effects that this may have. As we have noted, although the initial stages of coniferous afforestation can lead to a diversification of wildlife, it eventually supports a very limited bird community and in addition, it may cause irreparable damage to soils.

In an attempt to control the demands that society makes on Lakeland's natural resources, the Lake District National Park is charged with the task of conserving and enhancing its 'natural beauty', but too often this is equated with picturesque scenery, the maintenance of which is very different from conserving the natural environment. This was well demonstrated recently when British Nuclear Fuels Limited sought permission to raise the lake level of Wastwater by several feet and increase the quantity of water that they extract.

The idea of even a marginal alteration to the visual attractions of Wasdale caused such a massive public outcry that BNFL's proposal was eventually thwarted; yet it would be difficult to conceive of successfully motivating a similar number of people to protest at the activities of, say, the North West Water Authority, whose flood prevention measures have drastic effects upon the wildlife in and around Lakeland's rivers, but continue virtually unopposed.

Conservation of the natural environment can be achieved in a variety of ways, from the preservation of a special habitat, community or species by positive management which interferes with natural processes of change, to a laissez-faire policy, where nature is allowed to take its course without human interference until a climax is reached. To many people, non-management of this type is consistent with mis-management, since the resultant growth of vegetation appears untidy to them, or it restricts their access to the fellsides; yet it can be an effective way of restoring a semi-wild landscape. Another possibility is to create artificial 'wilderness' areas, although there is nothing new about this—one of Lakeland's most popular attractions, Tarn Hows, is almost entirely man-made; the tarn owes its existence to a dam built in 1865, and the islands and shore have been planted with coniferous species such as Scots Pine, larch and fir.

Positive conservation of any kind, however, can only occur if the considerable sums currently invested in upland agriculture and forestry are diverted to achieve social and ecological objectives, instead of the purely economic goals of the present system. There is otherwise a strong likelihood that a large part of Lakeland's natural heritage will be sacrificed to a so-called quality of life based upon an ideology of expansion and consumerism.

Wren

SYSTEMATIC LIST

Red-necked Grebe

Birds recorded in Cumbria since 1900, taken from the publications of the Carlisle Natural History Society and the Association of Natural History Societies in Cumbria (*see* Bibliography). There is a dearth of information concerning the period 1962-1973 and this list should not therefore be considered definitive.

Status Key

A	Abundant and widespread.
C	Common within favoured habitats.
U	Uncommon, often localised.
Sc	Scarce; residents very thinly distributed, migrants and visitors generally recorded annually.
O	Occasional; not recorded annually.
R	Rare; very infrequent occurrence, ( ) indicates species not recorded in last 20 years.
*	Feral birds frequently occur.

	Resident	Summer visitor	Migrant	Winter visitor	Vagrant	Primary habitat
Red-throated Diver				U	U	Coastal waters
Black-throated Diver				Sc		Inland and coastal waters
Great Northern Diver				Sc		Coastal waters
Pied-billed Grebe					R	Inland waters
Little Grebe	C			C		Inland waters
Great Crested Grebe	C			C		Inland and coastal waters
Red-necked Grebe				Sc		Coastal and inland waters
Slavonian Grebe				Sc		Coastal and inland waters
Black-necked Grebe				Sc		Coastal and inland waters
Fulmar	U	C	C	U		Coastal cliffs/Offshore
Cory's Shearwater			O			Offshore
Great Shearwater			O			Offshore
Sooty Shearwater			O			Offshore
Manx Shearwater		U				Offshore

	Resident	Summer visitor	Migrant	Winter visitor	Vagrant	Primary habitat
..... Wilson's Petrel					(R)	Offshore
..... Storm Petrel			Sc			Offshore
..... Leach's Petrel			O			Offshore
..... Gannet			U			Offshore
..... Cormorant		C	U	C		Coastal cliffs and waters
..... Shag			Sc	U		Offshore
..... Bittern				O		Reed fen
..... Night Heron					R	Rivers
..... Little Egret					R	Estuaries
..... Grey Heron	C					Estuaries/Inland waters
..... White Stork					R	Farmland
..... Glossy Ibis					(R)	Shallow waters
..... Spoonbill					R	Estuaries
..... Mute Swan	C					Inland waters
..... Berwick's Swan				O		Estuaries/Lakes
..... Whooper Swan				U		Lakes/Estuaries
..... Bean Goose				O		Saltmarshes
..... Pink-footed Goose				C		Saltmarshes
..... White-fronted Goose				O		Farmland
..... *Lesser White-fronted Goose					R	
..... Greylag Goose	C		U	U		Saltmarsh/Lakes/Farmland
..... *Snow Goose			R			
..... Canada Goose	U					Inland waters
..... Barnacle Goose				C		Solway marshes
..... Brent Goose				O		Estuaries
..... *Red-breasted Goose					(R)	
..... *Egyptian Goose	?					Saltmarshes
..... *Ruddy Shelduck					(R)	
..... Shelduck	C	except for autumn moult migration				Estuaries
..... *Mandarin	?			O		Inland waters
..... Wigeon	Sc		C	C		Estuaries
..... Gadwall	Sc		U	U		Estuaries/Inland waters
..... Teal	U		C	C		Saltmarshes/Inland waters
..... Mallard	C		U	U		Estuaries/Lakes
..... Pintail			U	U		Estuaries
..... Garganey		Sc	O			Inland waters
..... Shoveler		Sc	U	Sc		Estuaries/Inland waters
..... Pochard	Sc		U	C		Inland waters
..... Ring-necked Duck					R	
..... Tufted Duck	U		U	C		Inland waters
..... Scaup			U	U		Coastal waters
..... Eider	U			C		Coastal waters
..... King Eider					R	

Species	Resident	Summer visitor	Migrant	Winter visitor	Vagrant	Primary habitat
Long-tailed Duck			Sc	Sc		Coastal waters
Common Scoter		Sc	C	U		Offshore
Velvet Scoter			Sc	Sc		Offshore
Goldeneye	Sc		U	C		Estuaries/Lakes
Smew				Sc		Inland waters
Red-breasted Merganser	C		U	U		Coastal waters/Lakes
Goosander	U			C		Lakes and rivers
Ruddy Duck					Sc	Inland waters
Honey Buzzard		(R)				
Red Kite	R			R		
White-tailed Eagle					(R)	
Marsh Harrier	O	Sc				Reed fen
Hen Harrier		U	U			Coastal marshes/Moorland
Montagu's Harrier		R	R			
Goshawk	R				R	Woodlands
Sparrowhawk	C		U	U		Woodlands
Buzzard	C					Woodlands/Fellsides
Rough-legged Buzzard			O	O		
Golden Eagle	R					Mountains
Osprey		Sc				Inland waters
Kestrel	C	Sc	U			Fellsides/Farmland
Red-footed Falcon					(R)	
Merlin	Sc	U	U	U		Moorlands/Estuaries/Farmland
Hobby		R	R			
Gyr Falcon					(R)	
Peregrine	U		U	U		Crags/Estuaries
Red Grouse	C					Moorlands
Black Grouse	Sc					Moorlands/Upland forests
Capercaillie	?					Coniferous forest
Red-legged Partridge	U					Farmland
Partridge	C					Farmland
Quail		R	R			Farmland
Pheasant	C					Farmland/Woodland
Water Rail	U			U		Reed fen/Mire
Spotted Crake		R	R			Reed fen/Mire
Little Crake					(R)	
Corncrake		O	Sc			Farmland
Moorhen	C					Inland waters/Mire
Coot	C			C		Lakes and tarns
Crane					R	
Oystercatcher	C		C	C		Open shore/Saltmarsh
Avocet			R			Estuaries
Stone Curlew		R				

Capercaillie and Red-legged Partridge: } Recent introductions

	Resident	Summer visitor	Migrant	Winter visitor	Vagrant	Primary habitat
..... Cream-coloured Courser					(R)	
..... Pratincole					R	
..... Little Ringed Plover		Sc	Sc			Shingle shores on inland waters
..... Ringed Plover	C	C	C	C		Shingle and sandy shores
..... Dotterel		Sc	Sc			High fells/Coastal areas
..... Golden Plover	U	U	U	U		Moorlands/Saltmarsh/Farmland
..... Grey Plover			U	U		Estuaries
..... Lapwing	C	C	C	C		Farmland/Moorland/Saltmarsh
..... Knot			C	C		Intertidal areas
..... Sanderling			C	U		Sandy shores
..... Little Stint			Sc	R		Intertidal areas
..... Temminck's Stint			R			Freshwater pools
..... White-rumped Sandpiper			R			
..... Baird's Sandpiper					R	
..... Pectoral Sandpiper			R			
..... Curlew Sandpiper			Sc			Estuaries
..... Purple Sandpiper			U	U		Rocky coastline
..... Dunlin	U	U	C	C		Intertidal areas
..... Buff-breasted Sandpiper					R	
..... Ruff			U			Estuaries
..... Jack Snipe			U	U		Saltmarshes/Mire
..... Snipe	C		C	C		Saltmarshes/Mire
..... Great Snipe			(R)			
..... Woodcock	U		U	C		Woodlands/Mire
..... Black-tailed Godwit		R	U			Estuaries
..... Bar-tailed Godwit			U	U		Estuaries
..... Whimbrel			U			Coastal areas
..... Curlew	U	C	C	C		Moorlands/Estuaries
..... Spotted Redshank			Sc	O		Estuaries/Freshwater pools
..... Redshank	C	C	C	C		Saltmarshes
..... Greenshank			U	Sc		Estuaries/Freshwater pools
..... Green Sandpiper			Sc	O		Estuaries/Freshwater pools
..... Wood Sandpiper			O			Estuaries/Freshwater pools
..... Common Sandpiper		C	C			Inland waters/Rivers/Estuaries
..... Turnstone			U	U		Rocky coastline
..... Red-necked Phalarope		O	O			Estuaries
..... Grey Phalarope			O	R		Estuaries
..... Pomarine Skua			O	R		Offshore
..... Arctic Skua			U			Offshore
..... Long-tailed Skua			(R)			Offshore
..... Great Skua			Sc	O		Offshore
..... Mediterranean Gull			R	R		Coastal waters
..... Laughing Gull					R	

	Resident	Summer visitor	Migrant	Winter visitor	Vagrant	Primary habitat
..... Little Gull			O	O		Coastal and inland waters
..... Sabine's Gull			R	R		Coastal waters
..... Black-headed Gull	C		C	C		Coastal areas/Tarns/Lakes
..... Ring-billed Gull					R	
..... Common Gull		Sc	C	C		Estuaries/Lakes
..... Lesser Black-backed Gull	Sc	C	C	Sc		Coastal areas/Lakes
..... Herring Gull	C		U	C		Coastal areas
..... Iceland Gull				O		Coastal areas
..... Glaucous Gull				Sc		Coastal areas
..... Great Black-backed Gull	U		U	U		Coastal areas
..... Kittiwake		C	C	Sc		Coastal cliffs/Offshore
..... Sandwich Tern		C	C			Dunes/Offshore
..... Roseate Tern		Sc	O			Coastal areas
..... Common Tern		U	U			Dunes/Offshore
..... Arctic Tern		U	U			Dunes/Offshore
..... Sooty Tern		(R)				
..... Little Tern		Sc	Sc			Shingle shores/Coastal waters
..... Whiskered Tern			(R)			
..... Black Tern			Sc			Inland waters
..... White-winged Black Tern			(R)			
..... Guillemot	C					Coastal cliffs/Offshore
..... Razorbill	C					Coastal cliffs/Offshore
..... Black Guillemot	Sc					Coastal cliffs/Offshore
..... Little Auk				O		Offshore
..... Puffin	U					Coastal cliffs/Offshore
..... Stock Dove	C					Coastal cliffs/Inland crags
..... Woodpigeon	C			C	A	Woodlands/Farmland
..... Collared Dove	U					Near settlements
..... Turtle Dove		Sc	Sc			Farmland
..... Great Spotted Cuckoo				(R)		
..... Cuckoo		C	C			Fellsides/Dales
..... Barn Owl	U					Fellsides/Farmland
..... Scops Owl				(R)		
..... Snowy Owl				(R)		
..... Little Owl	U					Fellsides/Farmland/Quarries
..... Tawny Owl	C					Woodlands
..... Long-eared Owl	Sc		Sc	Sc		Coniferous forests
..... Short-eared Owl	Sc	Sc	Sc	U		Moors/Plantations/Coastal areas
..... Nightjar		U				Mooses/Fellsides
..... Swift		C	C			Near settlements/High fells
..... Alpine Swift				(R)		
..... Kingfisher	Sc					Rivers and lakes
..... Bee-eater					R	

	Resident	Summer visitor	Migrant	Winter visitor	Vagrant	*Primary habitat*
..... Roller					R	
..... Hoopoe			O			Farmland and gardens
..... Wryneck			Sc			
..... Green Woodpecker	C					Woodlands
..... Great Spotted Woodpecker	C					Woodlands
..... Lesser Spotted Woodpecker	Sc					Woodlands and gardens
..... Sand Martin		C	C			Sandy banks and cliffs
..... Swallow		C	C			Near settlements/Inland waters
..... House Martin		C	C			Near settlements/Inland waters
..... Shore Lark			O	O		
..... Wood Lark					(R)	
..... Skylark	C		C	C		Fellsides/Saltmarshes
..... Richard's Pipit			O			
..... Tawny Pipit			O			
..... Tree Pipit		C	C			Deciduous woodlands
..... Meadow Pipit	A		C	C		Fellsides/Saltmarsh
..... Red-throated Pipit			R			
..... Water/Rock Pipit	U			U		Coastal cliffs/Saltmarshes
..... Yellow Wagtail		U	U			Meadows/Farmland
..... Grey Wagtail	U	C	C			Rivers/Mountain streams
..... White/Pied Wagtail	C	C	O			Fellsides/Dales
..... Red-backed Shrike		O	O			Woodland margins/Mosses
..... Woodchat Shrike			R			
..... Great Grey Shrike				Sc		Scattered woodland/Mosses
..... Golden Oriole		O	O			Scattered deciduous woodland
..... Starling	A		A	A		Widespread
..... Jay	C					Woodland
..... Magpie	C			U		Dales/Farmland
..... Nutcracker					R	
..... Chough					Sc	Sea cliffs/Coastal areas
..... Jackdaw	C					Farmland/Crags
..... Rook	C			C		Farmland
..... Carrion Crow	C					Fellsides/Farmland
..... Raven	U					Mountains
..... Waxwing			O			Gardens
..... Dipper	C					Streams and rivers
..... Wren	A					Ubiquitous
..... Dunnock	C					Widespread
..... Savi's Warbler		O				Reed fen
..... Grasshopper Warbler		U	U			Mosses/Reed fen
..... Sedge Warbler		U	U			Reed fen/Thickets
..... Paddyfield Warbler					R	
..... Reed Warbler		Sc	O			Reed fen

						Primary habitat
	Resident	Summer visitor	Migrant	Winter visitor	Vagrant	
..... Icterine Warbler			O			
..... Melodious Warbler			O			
..... Barred Warbler					R	
..... Garden Warbler		C	C			Deciduous woods/Scrub
..... Blackcap		U	U	Sc		Deciduous woods/Scrub/Gardens
..... Whitethroat		C	C			Scrub
..... Lesser Whitethroat		Sc	Sc			Scrub/Open woodland
..... Willow Warbler		A	C			Deciduous woodland
..... Chiffchaff		C	C	O		Deciduous woodland
..... Bonelli's Warbler		R				
..... Wood Warbler		C				Open deciduous woodland
..... Yellow-browed Warbler				O		
..... Pallas's Warbler					R	
..... Goldcrest	C		C	C		Coniferous and mixed woodland
..... Firecrest			Sc	O		Mixed woodland
..... Pied Flycatcher		C	U			Open deciduous woodland
..... Red-breasted Flycatcher		R				
..... Spotted Flycatcher		C	U			Deciduous woodland/Gardens
..... Whinchat		U	U			Fellsides
..... Stonechat	U		Sc			Coastal scrub/Fellsides
..... Wheatear		C	C			Fellsides
..... Black Redstart			Sc	O		Coastal areas
..... Redstart		C	U			Deciduous woodland/Gardens
..... Robin	A		C			Ubiquitous in lowlands
..... Bluethroat			R			
..... Fieldfare			C	C		Farmland/Fellsides
..... Ring Ousel		U	U			Mountains
..... Blackbird	A	C	C	C		Ubiquitous below 400m
..... Redwing			C	C		Farmland/Scattered woodland
..... Song Thrush	C	C	U	C		Widespread below 500m
..... Mistle Thrush	C	C	C	C		Widespread below 500m
..... American Robin					R	
..... Bearded Tit				O		Reed fen
..... Long-tailed Tit	C					Woodlands/Thickets
..... Marsh Tit	Sc					Deciduous woodland and scrub
..... Willow Tit	U					Deciduous and mixed woodland
..... Crested Tit					R	
..... Coal Tit	C		U			Coniferous and mixed woodland
..... Blue Tit	A					Woodlands/Gardens
..... Great Tit	C					Woodlands/Gardens
..... Nuthatch	Sc					Deciduous woodland
..... Treecreeper	C					Mixed woodland
..... House Sparrow	C					Around settlements

76

	Resident	Summer visitor	Migrant	Winter visitor	Vagrant	*Primary habitat*
..... Tree Sparrow	U					Dales/Around settlements
..... Chaffinch	A		U	C		Widespread up to 500m
..... Brambling				Sc		Farmland/Gardens
..... Greenfinch	U			U		Gardens/Open woodland
..... Siskin	Sc			U		Mixed woodland, esp. conifers
..... Goldfinch	U					Waste ground/Hedgerows
..... Twite	Sc			U		Fellsides/Saltmarsh
..... Linnet	U			U		Fellsides/Coastal areas
..... Redpoll	U		U	U		Fellsides/Woodlands
..... Scarlet Rosefinch					R	
..... Crossbill	Sc			O		Coniferous woodland, esp. Pine
..... Two-barred Crossbill					R	
..... Bullfinch	U					Woodlands/Gardens
..... Hawfinch	Sc			O		Deciduous woodland/Gardens
..... Corn Bunting	U					Coastal areas/Farmland
..... Yellowhammer	C					Dales and fellsides up to 400m
..... Cirl Bunting		(R)	(R)			
..... Little Bunting					(R)	
..... Reed Bunting	C					Reed fens/Mosses/Farmland
..... Lapland Bunting			O	O		
..... Snow Bunting				Sc		Fellsides, esp. above 400m/Coast

ADDRESSES

Membership of the following two societies is strongly recommended:

Royal Society for the Protection of Birds
The Lodge, Sandy, Bedfordshire SG19 2DL

Cumbria Trust for Nature Conservation
Rydal Road, Ambleside, Cumbria LA22 9AN

Also, I would like to urge all readers to submit their birdwatching records to the County Recorder for inclusion in the annual publication *Birds in Cumbria*. This is *not* a journal of rare birds, but an attempt to provide a full account of the status of *all* birds seen in Cumbria. It is therefore of the utmost importance that we all contribute. There are relatively few resident birders in Cumbria, so records from visitors are especially important. The recorder is Malcolm Hutcheson, Gardener's Cottage, Sizergh Castle, Kendal, Cumbria LA8 8AE.

If you wish to participate even more actively in bird study, join the

British Trust for Ornithology
Beech Grove, Station Road, Tring, Hertfordshire HP23 5NR

Other useful addresses:

National Trust
Broadlands, Borrans Road, Ambleside, Cumbria LA22 0EJ

Cumbria Tourist Board
Ellerthwaite, Windermere, Cumbria LA23 2AQ

Forestry Commission
Grizedale, Hawkshead, Ambleside, Cumbria LA22 0QJ

Nature Conservancy Council
19 Belgrave Square, London SW1X 8PY or North West Regional Office, Blackwell, Bowness, Cumbria LA23 3JR

Fell Top Weather Service
Tel. Windermere 5151

Tide Tables
From Duddon Books, 2 St George's Road, Millom, and other booksellers

Mountain Goat Minibus Service
Victoria Street, Windermere. Tel. Windermere 5161

Cumberland Motor Services Limited
Head Office and timetable enquiries: Tangier Street, Whitehaven CA28 7XF. Tel. Whitehaven 63222/7

Ribble Bus Company
Local bus and coach information: Kendal Bus Station. Tel. Kendal 20932

Ravenglass and Eskdale Railway
Ravenglass, Cumbria. Tel. Ravenglass 226

BIBLIOGRAPHY

Allen, S E (Ed): *Natural History of the District around Grange-over-Sands* (Grange and District Natural History Society, 1975)

Brown, R H: *Lakeland Birdlife 1920-1970* (Published 1974)

Carlisle Natural History Society: *Birds of Lakeland* (1943)
  Lakeland Natural History (1946)
  Lakeland Ornithology (1954)
  Birds of the Lake Counties (1962)

Cumbria Trust for Nature Conservation: *Eskmeals Dunes Nature Reserve* (1976)
  South Walney Nature Reserve (1971)
  and Walney Bird Observatory Reports

ECOS: *Report on Forestry* Vol 3 no 1 (British Association of Nature Conservationists, 1982)

Hardy, E: *The Naturalist in Lakeland* (David and Charles, 1973)

Hervey, G E K and Barnes, J A G (Eds): *Natural History of the Lake District* (Warne, 1970)

Hutchinson, M (Sub Ed): *Natural History in Cumbria* and *Birds in Cumbria* 1973-1985 (Association of Natural History Societies in Cumbria)

MacEwen, A & M: *National Parks: Conservation or Cosmetics* (Allen and Unwin, 1982)

Macpherson, Rev H A: *A Vertebrate Fauna of Lakeland* (David Douglas, 1892; Reprinted Paul Minet, 1972)

Macpherson, Rev H A and Duckworth, William: *The Birds of Cumberland* (Turnham, 1886)

Mitchell, W R and Robson, R W: *Lakeland Birds* (Dalesman, 1974)

Oakes, C: *The Birds of Lancashire* (Oliver and Boyd, 1953)

Pearsall, W H and Pennington, W: *The Lake District* (Collins New Naturalist, 1973)

Philipson, W R: *Birds of a Valley* (Longman, 1948)

Wilson, J: *Birds of Morecambe Bay* (Dalesman)

Also:

Bassenthwaite Lake—a Discussion Paper on Future Management (Lake District Special Planning Board)

The Greylag's Return (Cumbria Magazine, Jan 1982; Dalesman)

St Bees Head Records 1978-1982 (RSPB)

West Cumbria Field Society Annual Transactions 1976

ACKNOWLEDGEMENTS

I would like to thank the following organisations for their assistance and information: RSPB, CTNC, Lake District National Park Planning Board, National Park Visitor Centre, Forestry Commission, National Trust, Cumbria County Council and the Ordnance Survey. I also thank Chatto and Windus Ltd for permission to use lines from Norman MacCaig's poem "Greenshank" on the title page.

I am greatly indebted to many individuals for their help and encouragement, especially Annabel Riley, Fay Wilkinson, Jim Ellwood, Lynne Fox, Sally Morris, and most of all, David and Janet Woodhead for checking the original manuscript, offering sound advice and furthering my bird book collection. It also seems appropriate here to mention Merlyn, companion on all my walks in the 'wide open spaces'.

M. M.

Many people have greatly assisted my illustrative efforts, both directly and indirectly, and unfortunately space (and memory) prevents me from thanking them all.

Thanks are especially due, of course, to Mike Madders, for introducing me to Cumbria and its birds; to Barry Barnacal, and the Manchester Polytechnic staff, for their generous technical expertise; to Raymond Ching, Terence Lambert and Pollyanna Pickering, for their encouragement and advice; to the myriad exponents of black-and-white illustration, especially the masterly C F Tunnicliffe; to my parents for my good eyesight and I-Spy books; to Ralph, who—although lacking Merlyn's lineage—is unparalleled at pointing Dunnock and rubbish bags; and to Maraji, who brought it all together for me.

P. S.